CRE🏠TIVE
HOMEOWNER®

ULTIMATE GUIDE
DRYWALL

CRE▲TIVE
HOMEOWNER®

ULTIMATE GUIDE
DRYWALL

CREATIVE HOMEOWNER®, Upper Saddle River, New Jersey

ULTIMATE GUIDE: DRYWALL

MANAGING EDITOR	Fran Donegan
EDITOR	Lisa Kahn
GRAPHIC DESIGNER	Kathryn Wityk
PHOTO COORDINATOR	Mary Dolan
JUNIOR EDITOR	Angela Hanson
PROOFREADER	Sara M. Markowitz
DIGITAL IMAGING SPECIALIST	Frank Dyer
INDEXER	Schroeder Indexing Services
COVER DESIGN	Kathryn Wityk
FRONT COVER PHOTOGRAPY	David Baer of Smith-Baer Studios
BACK COVER PHOTOGRAPY	John Parsekian/CH

CREATIVE HOMEOWNER

VICE PRESIDENT AND PUBLISHER	Timothy O. Bakke
ART DIRECTOR	David Geer
MANAGING EDITOR	Fran J. Donegan
PRODUCTION COORDINATOR	Sara M. Markowitz

Manufactured in the United States of America

Current Printing (last digit)
10 9 8 7 6 5 4 3

Ultimate Guide: Drywall, Third Edition
Library of Congress Control Number: 2010921121
ISBN-10: 1-58011-500-4
ISBN-13: 978-1-58011-500-1

CREATIVE HOMEOWNER®
A Division of Federal Marketing Corp.
24 Park Way
Upper Saddle River, NJ 07458
www.creativehomeowner.com

5156 3996
4/13

Planet Friendly Publishing
✓ Made in the United States
✓ Printed on Recycled Paper
Text: 10%   Cover: 10%
Learn more: www.greenedition.org

GREEN EDITION®

safety

Although the methods in this book have been reviewed for safety, it is not possible to overstate the importance of using the safest methods you can. What follows are reminders—some do's and don'ts of work safety—to use along with your common sense.

- Always use caution, care, and good judgment when following the procedures described in this book.
- Always be sure that the electrical setup is safe, that no circuit is overloaded, and that all power tools and outlets are properly grounded. Do not use power tools in wet locations.
- Always read container labels on paints, solvents, and other products; provide ventilation; and observe all other warnings.
- Always read the manufacturer's instructions for using a tool, especially the warnings.
- Use hold-downs and push sticks whenever possible when working on a table saw. Avoid working short pieces if you can.
- Always remove the key from any drill chuck (portable or press) before starting the drill.
- Always pay deliberate attention to how a tool works so that you can avoid being injured.
- Always know the limitations of your tools. Do not try to force them to do what they were not designed to do.
- Always make sure that any adjustment is locked before proceeding. For example, always check the rip fence on a table saw or the bevel adjustment on a portable saw before starting to work.
- Always clamp small pieces to a bench or other work surface when using a power tool.
- Always wear the appropriate rubber gloves or work gloves when handling chemicals, moving or stacking lumber, working with concrete, or doing heavy construction.
- Always wear a disposable face mask when you create dust by sawing or sanding. Use a special filtering respirator when working with toxic substances and solvents.
- Always wear eye protection, especially when using power tools or striking metal on metal or concrete; a chip can fly off, for example, when chiseling concrete.
- Never work while wearing loose clothing, open cuffs, or jewelry; tie back long hair.
- Always be aware that there is seldom enough time for your body's reflexes to save you from injury from a power tool in a dangerous situation; everything happens too fast. Be alert!
- Always keep your hands away from the business ends of blades, cutters, and bits.
- Always hold a circular saw firmly, usually with both hands.
- Always use a drill with an auxiliary handle to control the torque when using large-size bits.
- Always check your local building codes when planning new construction. The codes are intended to protect public safety and should be observed to the letter.
- Never work with power tools when you are tired or when under the influence of alcohol or drugs.
- Never cut tiny pieces of wood or pipe using a power saw. When you need a small piece, saw it from a securely clamped longer piece.
- Never change a saw blade or a drill or router bit unless the power cord is unplugged. Do not depend on the switch being off. You might accidentally hit it.
- Never work in insufficient lighting.
- Never work with dull tools. Have them sharpened, or learn how to sharpen them yourself.
- Never use a power tool on a workpiece—large or small—that is not firmly supported.
- Never saw a workpiece that spans a large distance between horses without close support on each side of the cut; the piece can bend, closing on and jamming the blade, causing saw kickback.
- When sawing, never support a workpiece from underneath with your leg or other part of your body.
- Never carry sharp or pointed tools, such as utility knives, awls, or chisels, in your pocket. If you want to carry any of these tools, use a special-purpose tool belt that has leather pockets and holders.

Contents

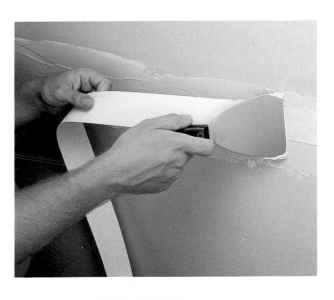

Introduction

THIS BOOK IS WRITTEN for the do-it-yourselfer who brings beginning to intermediate building skills to dry-walling projects large and small. The book is designed to walk the reader through the basics of installing gypsum drywall, step by step, from estimating, cutting, hanging, and finishing drywall panels to making basic repairs.

Of all the ways that you can finish the interior of your home—including plaster, wood paneling, and brick—gyp-sum drywall is not only the least expensive but also the simplest to install. Anyone with more than a passing familiarity with simple tools, such as a power drill, hand-saw, hammer, utility knife, and measuring tape, should, with a little patience, be able to hang drywall just as neatly (although not nearly as quickly) as a team of professional drywall contractors.

After two introductory chapters that show you the basics of the materials and the tools involved in a normal residential drywall project, Chapter 3, "Preparing to Dry-wall," deals with the important issues of estimating materials, making efficient layouts, and preparing the house framing for flawless drywalling. Chapter 4, "Cutting Dry-wall," analyzes the many methods for cutting drywall panels—including circles, archways, and other irregular

Drywall Hanging Skills. Most drywalling tasks involve ordinary skills—hammering nails, cutting panels, and sanding, for example.

lines. Chapter 5, "Installing Drywall," deals with actually hanging the panels, covering not just the basics (flat walls and ceilings) but myriad potential problem situations, such as curved walls, cathedral ceilings, and drywalling over steel framing. Chapter 6, "Taping & Finishing," covers not just the basics of spreading compound, taping, and sanding down panels, but also specialty finishes. Chapter 7, "Repairing Drywall," contains numerous suggestions for making repairs—simple and complex—to drywall that has been damaged in some way.

This edition includes more-advanced drywall projects that go beyond the basics of installing panels on walls or ceilings. The projects add a unique look to any room. The book closes with a section on the "Recommended Levels of Drywall Finish," which details how the final finish you plan to apply might affect your drywall project.

GUIDE TO SKILL LEVEL

 Easy. Even for beginners

 Challenging. Can be done by beginners who have the patience and willingness to learn.

 Difficult. Can be handled by most experienced do-it-yourselfers who have mastered basic construction skills. Consider consulting a specialist.

Unique Designs. While most drywall surfaces are flat, unusual designs are possible with drywall. See pages 61 to 63 and 146 to 159 for examples.

Cutting and Installing. Drywall is easy to work—cut panels using a sharp utility knife and a straightedge; attach the panels using nails or screws; and conceal the seams using tape and drywall joint compound.

1 drywall fundamentals

DRYWALL, ALSO KNOWN AS PLASTERBOARD, wallboard, or gypsum board, is by

far the most popular and practical material for surfacing interior walls. Nowadays it's rare

to find a finished wall, either in a home or a business, that hasn't been surfaced with

some kind of drywall product. Drywall is durable, easy to finish with paint or wallpaper,

simple to repair, and you don't need to be an expert to install it. Perfectly flat, plumb

walls are within the reach of any handy, patient homeowner willing to invest the time.

HISTORY OF DRYWALL

Before drywall was developed in the 1930s, plaster was the most widely used wallcovering and the only economical alternative to expensive solid wood paneling.

Plaster can be extremely durable—some plaster walls have survived for hundreds of years—but it tends to be brittle unless it's applied over a truly rigid frame. Older homes (generally pre-World War II) were structured for plaster. They were built using a system called balloon framing, which called for long lengths of full-size 2×4 studs that ran from the foundation to the roof rafters.

Since then, contractors have preferred framing one floor at a time using shorter studs. This more economical platform system yielded a strong frame but less rigid walls, which created the need for a sturdier wall-covering—one of the many reasons for the development of drywall.

Labor time became a factor as well. Builders nailed wooden lath to the studs and joists, and then applied plaster to the lath in a three-coat process. The first coat, called the scratch coat, was forced into the gaps, locking itself to the lath. The brown coat covered the scratch coat, and the thin white coat went on last for finish. The process was tedious and lath did not always present a flat surface.

Eventually the twin economic pressures of labor and material began to put the squeeze on plaster. Builders were demanding a wallcovering that went up easily, required no lathing, and presented a flat surface without painstaking finish work.

What Is Drywall? Rock-solid walls begin, appropriately, with rock—namely, the mineral gypsum. Powdered, mixed with water, and poured between sheets of paper, gypsum forms the solid core of a drywall panel.

In the early 1930s, United States Gypsum Company (USG) invented Rocklath, a paper-and-gypsum board that attached to the studs as an underlayment. The plaster bonded directly to it, making plastering a little faster and easier, but the job still took a lot of time even without nailing up lath.

The First Drywall

Near the end of the 1930s, USG developed the Sheetrock Drywall System—thicker gypsum panels that could be taped together neatly and required no plaster top coat. Although it wasn't used widely until the postwar housing boom, Sheetrock evolved into the more refined paper-coated gypsum board that covers the walls and ceilings of most homes today.

PLASTER VS DRYWALL

Drywall: The "Modern Plaster." Plaster walls (left) consist of a lath base and a scratch coat, a brown coat, and a finish coat of plaster. Drywall (right) has largely replaced plaster because of its ease of installation and low cost.

Plaster

Lath

Scratch Coat

Brown Coat

Finish Coat

2x4

Drywall

½" Drywall

2x4

Drywall Fundamentals

Gypsum drywall is converted rock: it starts out as calcium sulfate dihydrate, or hydrous calcium sulfate ($CaSO_4 \cdot 2H_2O$), also known as gypsum, a mineral that ranges from almost black to white in color. As the chemical formula indicates, gypsum naturally contains water. In fact, water makes up about 21 percent of gypsum's weight and about 50 percent of its volume as water of crystallization. This is what gives drywall its fire resistance. The crystallized water in gypsum will turn to steam when exposed to extreme heat, keeping fire from spreading and the temperature down for a limited period of time.

The gypsum, once mined, is crushed, dried, and ground to a powder. This powder is then heated to drive off most of the remaining carbon dioxide and water, at which point it has been dehydrated to form calcium sulfate hemihydrate ($CaSO_4 \cdot \frac{1}{2}H_2O$), better known as Plaster of Paris. This calcined gypsum is then mixed with water, which rehydrates it back into calcium sulfate dihydrate. The resulting slurry is poured between two sheets of heavy paper with folded edges, sandwiched flat, and allowed to set. The boards are then cut, dried, and (if they don't require a special finish) packaged for sale.

Finding Gypsum. Deposits occur in two large areas in the United States, as well as in Nova Scotia and Mexico.

BENEFITS OF DRYWALL

WHY USE GYPSUM WALLBOARD instead of plaster? Besides the time saved during its installation, drywall offers a number of other benefits: it's fire-resistant; it helps deaden sound; it's durable; and it's easy to repair. Specialty drywall (with foil faces and a fiberglass core) can have a fire-resistance rating of 4 hours or even higher, depending on its thickness. Drywall makes a home quieter because gypsum naturally resists sound transmission. It resists fracturing, withstands a good deal of typical household abuse, and can be repaired easily using drywall patches to mend holes or a simple application of joint compound to smooth out dings and dents.

In addition to these benefits, drywall's paper facing readily takes a number of finishes, including paint, texturing, and wallpaper. Certain drywall products (some of which contain no gypsum) can serve as an underlayment for tile. These water-resistant drywall and cementitious (cement-based) panels go by trade names such as Durock Cement Board.

HOW TO ORDER DRYWALL

HAVE YOUR DRYWALL DELIVERED only when you are ready to use it, after the framers are done and the wiring and plumbing have been roughed in. Panels get damaged if you store them on a job site for too long, especially if workers are walking through, carrying unwieldy tools and snaking extension cords.

Drywall is heavy. A 4 × 8-foot panel of ½-inch gypsum drywall weighs about 54 pounds. Panels are shipped as two-sheet units that are joined by a strip of paper at each end. One strong person can pick up a single sheet, but you'll want to recruit an assistant if you have to handle more than a few sheets.

If you order ten sheets or more, drywall is typically delivered on a boom truck with an articulated crane arm that can lift it to a second story. The crane arm cradles the drywall just outside the window for easy re-

Using a Boom Truck. This is the easiest way to get drywall into an upper floor. Above, a lumberyard's boom truck lifts panels to where they can be pulled through a second-story window.

moval. (Check to make sure the window area is clear of utility wires.) Window delivery decreases labor and eliminates the hazard of carrying panels up the stairs, which can damage or bow them, to say nothing of potential back injuries to the workers.

If possible, it's best to take delivery through a window before the jambs have been installed. If the windows are already in place and are large enough, remove the sashes to avoid potential damage. This will take some time, but it still beats carrying panels from the first floor up a narrow staircase.

For first-floor delivery, carry the panels through a doorway, or position the boom truck's crane near an open window and pass the panels through. If you have to carry stock through a finished or carpeted area, lay down plastic or plywood to protect the floor.

HOW TO STORE DRYWALL

WHEN STORING DRYWALL, distribute the panels throughout the house to spread the weight around—50 panels can weigh over a ton. Estimate the number and types of panels each room requires; that way, you can distribute them upon delivery and avoid double-handling.

If space is tight, stack panels on edge lengthwise against the wall that you will drywall last, with the good, or face, side out. Choose a location in which the panels can sit perpendicular to the floor joists to help distribute weight evenly. If you intend to lay your stock flat on the floor, sweep the area thoroughly beforehand to remove any debris that might press into the panels and cause a blemish, scratch, or dent. Always store panels back side down on the floor.

Don't place drywall on blocks. The panels will sag between blocks, and the resulting bows will make installation difficult later on. Once drywall is on site, keep the temperature between 55 and 70 degrees Fahrenheit.

GYPSUM DRYWALL SIZES & TYPES

Length

Gypsum drywall comes in 8-, 9-, 10-, 12-, 14-, and 16-foot lengths. It's best to use longer panels where possible to minimize the number of seams. Fewer seams mean less taping and less chance that irregular seams will show through the finished wall.

Width

Common gypsum drywall panels measure 48 inches wide. Two stacked horizontal pieces or one vertical 96-inch length will span 8 feet, the height of a common ceiling. With some ceiling heights now measuring 8½ or 9 feet high, manufacturers have started producing 54-inch-wide panels. Two of these will cover a 9-foot wall.

Long Drywall. The length of gypsum drywall goes far beyond the 8 ft. that most suppliers have in stock. Panels as long as 14 and 16 ft. are available to finish long walls with a minimal number of seams.

Thickness

Gypsum drywall comes in ¼-, ⅜-, ½-, and ⅝-inch thicknesses. Here's a look at common applications for each thickness.

- **¼-Inch-Thick Drywall:** Available in 8- and 10-foot panels, this stock is used for curved walls and sometimes for resurfacing over plaster or other solid-surface walls. Handle these panels carefully; because of their thinness, they can easily whip like sheet metal while being carried and can break apart. On curved walls, even a short length of ¼-inch-thick drywall requires a maximum stud spacing of 16 inches on center; it will noticeably bow on 24-inch on-center studs. When installing over a solid surface, use adhesive to help hold the panels in place. At 1.2 pounds per square foot, a 4 × 8-foot sheet of ¼-inch-thick drywall weighs about 38 pounds.

- **⅜-Inch-Thick Drywall:** Available in 8-, 9-, 10-, 12-, and 14-foot lengths, this material is ideal for remodeling partition walls and for patching areas where old plaster has been removed. A ⅜-inch thickness requires a maximum stud spacing of 16 inches on-center. At 1.4 pounds per square foot, a 4 × 8-foot panel weighs about 45 pounds.

- **½-Inch-Thick Drywall:** Available in 8-, 9-, 10-, 12-, 14-, and 16-foot lengths, this most common thickness works well for both walls and ceilings. Stud spacing can be 24 inches on center, unless the panels are hung with their long edges parallel with the ceiling joints. In this case, stick with 16-inch on-center framing to prevent sagging. At 1.7 pounds per square foot, a 4 × 8-foot sheet weighs about 54 pounds.

- **⅝-Inch-Thick Drywall:** Available in 8-, 9-, 10-, 12-, and 14-foot lengths, this stock, sometimes called firewall drywall, can be used in walls and ceilings. Like ½-inch, it can be hung on 24-inch on-center framing unless it is hung horizontally. The extra thickness improves sound dampening and resistance to sagging. In many areas, ⅝-inch drywall is required by code because of its superior fire resistance. At 2.3 pounds per square foot, a 4 × 8-foot panel weighs about 73 pounds.

- **Double-Layer Systems:** To increase a wall's fire resistance and sound-dampening qualities, you can apply a double layer of drywall. A double-layer application also offers superior resistance to sagging and cracking (especially when adhesives are used). The bottom, or base, layer is covered by a top, or face, layer. Typically, adhesive is used between layers.

DRYWALL PANELS

As discussed on page 14, drywall panels are available in a variety of sizes. The standard for most residential work is the ½-inch-thick panel. Larger ⅝-inch panels are not usually used in houses due to the extra weight and cost. It may not seem like much, but that extra ⅛ inch makes the larger panels much heavier and harder to handle, especially for someone working alone. The lighter ⅜-inch-thick panels are good for resurfacing work when a wall is so scarred that spackling cannot save it. The ¼-inch-thick panel is the most economical, but most people, including most pros, don't like to use them because the sheets are very whippy and snap too easily during handling. Of course, be sure to check local building codes when planning a large-scale new construction or remodeling project.

As is the case with plywood and other construction sheet goods, the standard size for drywall panels is 4 × 8 feet, although other sizes are available. (See "Gypsum Drywall Sizes and Types," opposite.) The standard size works well with both 16-inch and 24-inch-on-center framing.

Two common variations of standard panels are manufactured with qualities that improve drywall performance in key areas: panels impregnated with fire retardants, referred to as FC or fire code panels—see "Fire Resistant Drywall," page 17—and drywall panels that are treated to resist moisture—see "Dealing with Moisture," page 19.

From the standpoint of handling, smaller sheets are best—easier to carry and install. But from the standpoint of taping and finishing joints, larger sheets are better because they cover more wall area. The best approach is to use the largest sheets practicable—large enough to eliminate some seams and taping time but not large enough to create major handling problems.

Drywall Types: A—¼ in., B—⅜ in., C—½ in., D—⅝ in. fire code, E—½ in. water-resistant.

DRYWALL PANELS FOR SPECIAL USES

- **Flexible Drywall:** This ¼-inch-thick material is intended for tighter curved-wall or archway applications and is often applied in two layers. Flexible gypsum drywall has a stronger liner and face paper than regular ¼-inch-thick drywall and resists cracking more effectively.

- **Abuse-Resistant Drywall:** Compared with standard gypsum panels, abuse-resistant panels have a heavier paper covering and a reinforced core. These panels give greater resistance to damage. Available in ½- and ⅝-inch thicknesses, this stock is recommended for playrooms, high-traffic hallways, and garage and basement walls that are likely to sustain damage from bikes or tools. For this type of usage, manufacturers have recently developed a gypsum/wood fiber backing that resists dents and punctures better than paper and increases panel strength. Stock with this backing costs more than ordinary gypsum drywall and usually must be special-ordered.

- **Moisture-Resistant Drywall:** Also called MR (moisture-resistant) board, WR (water-resistant) board, green board, or blue board, this gypsum drywall (whichhas a pale green or blue face) resists moisture but is not waterproof. It can withstand the high levels of humidity that often occur in bathrooms, kitchens, and laundry rooms. These panels make a good base for any kind of tile attached with a mastic. Avoid hanging the material over an existing vapor barrier, because this would trap moisture, causing the drywall to degrade over time. Moisture-resistant drywall can be finished and painted or wallpapered like regular drywall panels. It should be installed on studs framed 16 inches on center.

Panels for Curves. Specially-made flexible panels cover curved walls and archways without requiring kerfing or soaking with water.

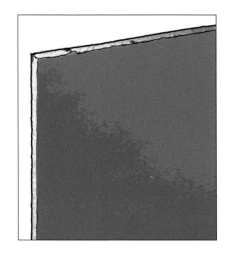

Flexible Drywall. Flexible ¼-in. drywall is a convenient product for curved walls and double-layered installations, but ordinary walls call for a thicker panel.

Abuse-Resistant Drywall. For rooms with lots of traffic or the potential for wall damage, abuse-resistant drywall can withstand moderate impacts without being damaged.

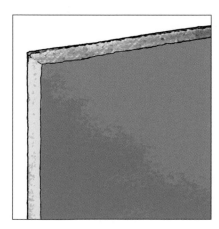

Moisture-Resistant Drywall. While not waterproof, this material is a good choice in high-humidity areas such as kitchens and bathrooms; it's used to support ceramic tile behind a kitchen sink, for example.

■ **Cement Board:** Also called cementitious panel, Durock, Hardibacker, WonderBoard, or DensShield, this ½- or ⅝-inch-thick stock comes in 5- or 8-foot lengths and in widths of 32, 36, and 48 inches. Unlike gypsum-based products, this material consists of a portland cement core sandwiched between layers of a polymer-coated glass fiber mesh. It provides excellent fire and water resistance and makes an ideal backing for tile, especially in high-moisture areas such as bathroom and kitchen walls and floors. It also offers a superior underlayment for use with slate and quarry tile. Each cement-based board has a rough and a smooth side. Install the rough side facing outward when attaching tiles with mortar (such as Quikrete) or with the smooth side out when using adhesive or mastic. Some cementitious products are UL-listed for use as wall shield and floor protectors in rooms with exposed heaters and wood stoves. Maximum stud spacing for application is 16 inches on center.

■ **Fire-Resistant Drywall:** Available in ½- and ⅝-inch thicknesses, this material, known as Firecode Core, Fire-Shield, Fireguard, or Fi-Rock, is fire resistant. This means that it meets or exceeds the ASTM C36 rating for Type X fire-resistant gypsum board, which specifies that glass fibers be embedded in its core, enabling it to resist fire for a certain amount of time beyond conventional gypsum drywall. Typically, a ½-inch-thick panel is rated to contain a fire for 45 minutes, a ⅝-inch-thick panel for 60 minutes. Codes often require these panels for party walls (between condos or apartments), for ceilings that adjoin other units, and for rooms that are susceptible to fire, such as furnace rooms, attached garages, and kitchens.

■ **Foil-Backed Board:** Where a vapor barrier is required, foil-backed panels may be useful. This stock is made by laminating aluminum foil (backed by kraft paper) to the surface of a gypsum drywall panel. The foil face increases the insulation value of the drywall and helps create a vapor barrier if the foil face is placed against the studs on the interior side of exterior walls. As with any vapor barrier, this helps prevent moisture in the living area from entering the stud bays. Avoid using foil-backed panels as a base for tiles or in any area where another wall covering could trap moisture within the core of the panel. Also, avoid using this material in air-conditioned structures that ordinarily withstand frequent high outdoor temperatures and humidity.

Cement Board. These panels are for areas that need extra resistance to fire or water damage. They are also an excellent tile backer for high-moisture areas such as bathroom and kitchen walls and as an underlayment for slate and quarry tile.

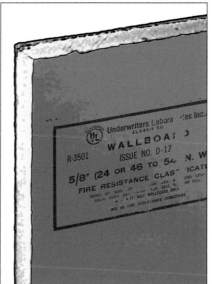

Fire-Resistant Drywall. These panels can contain a fire for a certain amount of time. Building codes often require fire-resistant panels in party walls between apartments or in common walls between a house and an attached garage.

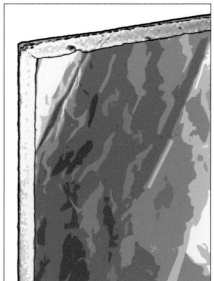

Foil-Backed Board. Many fire-resistant products have a kraft-backed aluminum foil layer. Besides preventing the spread of fire, the foil forms an excellent vapor barrier.

Drywall Fundamentals

■ **Sound-Deadening Board:** Sound-deadening in drywall application has more to do with wall design than with the use of any particular drywall product. Sound-deadening materials are available, but they usually are sold as insulation, such as USG's Thermafiber. Sound-deadening techniques typically combine the use of two layers of drywall with a sound-deadening blanket, an acoustical sealant, and a wall system of studs and metal channels that creates baffles within a wall.

■ **Ceiling Panels:** A number of manufacturers make special panels for use in ceiling applications, particularly when the ceiling is built with wider truss spans (24 inches on center). Designed to be both lighter and stronger than standard stock; these panels resist sagging, install more easily, and in some cases cost less than regular gypsum drywall.

■ **Vinyl-Faced Panels:** Available in a wide variety of colors and patterns, these gypsum drywall panels are attached using adhesive and special fasteners (similar to finishing nails) and require no edge or joint treatments because they're trimmed with specially designed vinyl moldings. Butted end joints are difficult to conceal, so avoid using these panels in rooms or on ceilings where end joints will be visible. Panels typically come in ½-inch thicknesses and in 4-, 8-, 9-, and 10-foot lengths.

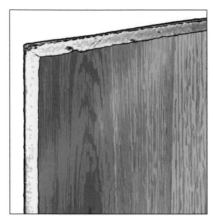

Vinyl-Faced Panels. These predecorated panels, usually seen in commercial settings, have a vinyl face that does not need to be painted. These panels are trimmed with plastic moldings rather than tape and joint compound.

■ **Gypsum Lath:** Gypsum lath serves as a base for veneer plaster. Sold under such names as Rocklath and Kal-Kore, gypsum lath provides a fire-resistant underlayment for trowel applications of plaster, replacing wooden lath. It comes in ½- and ⅜-inch thicknesses, with panel sizes ranging from 16 × 48 inches to 25 × 96 inches. Although not identical to drywall, gypsum lath can have a gypsum core and often is faced with absorbent paper. The paper draws water away from the freshly applied plaster to keep it from slumping, while several additional layers of treated paper prevent this moisture from seeping into the panel's core.

MOLDINGS FOR PREDECORATED PANELS

Decorative Trim. Special moldings finish the edges and joints where predecorated panels meet on the wall and at corners, and where the panels end. These panels are usually installed vertically.

DEALING WITH MOISTURE

Moisture damages drywall surfaces. Anyone who has ever experienced a leaky roof or pipe knows that the repair to the source of the leak is often followed up with a repair to the damaged wall or ceiling. Even minor leaks can, over time, cause paint to peel and the outer layer of paper on a standard drywall panel to delaminate. Excessive moisture can cause the panel to crumble.

For years drywall manufacturers have offered products designed for installation in high-moisture areas such as bathrooms and kitchens. (See "Drywall Panels for Special Uses," pages 16–18.) But tighter construction practices of recent years have led to additional moisture problems. In some homes, the increased levels of humidity generated by normal everyday activities such as cooking, drying clothes, and showering can lead to wet wall and ceiling surfaces and to the formation of mold. An undetected leak can also lead to the formation of mold. Mold spores will grow on any wet surface, including the back of wallpaper and drywall surfaces inside wall cavities.

Although it is unsightly, most molds are not dangerous to most people. However, many people are sensitive to mold

Waterproof Applications. A proper tile system that starts with waterproof cement-based backerboard is the secret to avoiding moisture problems in shower surrounds.

spores. Reactions can range from hay fever-type symptoms to more extreme reactions such as asthma attacks in people with asthma who are allergic to mold.

To help prevent the formation of mold, be sure your home is properly ventilated. Clothes dryers, kitchen ranges, and bathrooms should be vented to the outdoors. There are also products designed for increased water resistance.

Paperless Panels. Some manufacturers offer drywall panels that do not contain the typical paper facing. Removing the organic paper means there is nothing for mold spores to feed upon, nor is there the possibility of the paper pulling away from the gypsum core. Moisture will not affect these panels as it does typical drywall panels. Some manufacturers replace the paper with a glass-fiber matt; others use a gypsum formulation that provides a smooth surface. The new generation of paperless panels comes in standard sizes. Installation and finishing options are the same for new paperless panels as they are for traditional drywall panels.

VENTILATION BASICS

YOU CAN AVOID many moisture problems in new and remodeled homes through proper ventilation. Kitchens and bathrooms should contain ventilation systems that vent moisture and stale air directly outdoors. Ventilation fans are rated by the amount of air they move in cubic feet per minute (CFM).

Kitchens
Ranges and cooktops installed against a wall
    Light cooking: 40 CFM
    Medium to heavy cooking: 100 to 150 CFM

Ranges and cooktops installed in islands and peninsulas:
    Light cooking: 50 CFM
    Medium to heavy cooking: 150 to 300 CFM

Bathrooms
CFM = Room Width (feet) x Room Length (feet) x 1.1

DRYWALL FASTENERS

Drywall is attached to studs and joists with nails or screws. Screws have become the preferred fastener because they are easy to install, provide more holding power than nails, and don't disturb the framing or furring when applied. The pounding of drywall nails can shake furring loose, cause nails already in place to pop, and even move studs out of alignment. In addition, screws can be removed (in case you have to remove and recut a panel), and screwhead depth is easier to control, especially with screw-gun clutches that can be set to release once a screw has reached a desired depth. (Nailhead depth must be gauged correctly by eye every time.)

choosing nails & screws

Fastener Type	Drywall Thickness	Minimum Fastener Length
Type W screws *(coarse thread)*	⅜ in.	1 in.
	½ in.	1⅛ in.
	⅝ in.	1¼ in.
Type S screws *(self-tapping)*	⅜ in.	1 in.
	½ in.	1¼ in.
	⅝ in.	1⅜ in.
Ring-shank nails *(wooden studs only)*	⅜ in.	1⅛ in.
	½ in.	1¼ in.
	⅝ in.	1⅜ in.

TYPES OF NAILS

THERE ARE THREE TYPES OF NAILS used to fasten drywall to wooden studs and ceiling joists. Nail length varies according to the thickness of your drywall. For ⅜-inch-thick panels, use 1⅛-inch nails; for ½-inch, use 1¼-inch nails; for ⅝-inch, use 1⅜-inch nails. Drive the nails with a bell- or convex-faced drywall hammer. The wide, rounded crosshatched, heads on these hammers create a dimple around the nailhead that facilitates the application of joint compound. All nails are designed to attach drywall to wooden, not steel, studs. If you're attaching drywall to metal studs or furring strips, use screws.

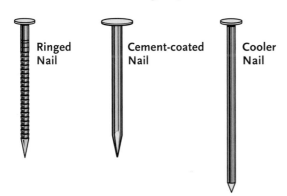

Ringed Nail / Cement-coated Nail / Cooler Nail

Three Types of Drywall Nails. Ringed nails (left) are threaded to resist pullout. Cement-coated nails (center) use cement coating to add friction to the nail's bite, defeating pullout. Cooler nails (right) are smooth-shank nails used in drywall applications where risk of pullout is not great.

TYPES OF SCREWS

THREE TYPES OF PHILLIPS-HEAD SCREWS are used to fasten drywall to studs and joists: Type W (wood), Type G (gypsum), and Type S (steel) screws. When fastening drywall to wood studs or joists, use **Type W screws.** Use **Type G screws** to fasten one drywall panel to another in a double-layer application. To fasten panels to metal studs or furring, use **Type S screws**—preferably self-tapping screws, which have winged tips that drill through steel quickly.

As with nails, drive the screws far enough to create a dimple, but don't tear the paper. (You can outfit a power drill with a clutch that will release the screw when it is driven to a certain depth.)

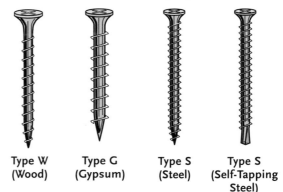

Type W (Wood) / Type G (Gypsum) / Type S (Steel) / Type S (Self-Tapping Steel)

Three Types of Drywall Screws. Type W screws are designed for attaching drywall to wood studs. Type G screws are for attaching drywall to drywall. Type S screws—normal and self-tapping—are designed for attaching drywall to steel studs.

ADHESIVES

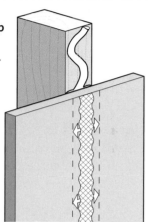

Drywall Adhesive. Using adhesive can help reduce the number of fasteners required to attach drywall. Drywall adhesive is properly applied in a bead form, and when the panel is pressed into place, the adhesive should flatten out across the face of the stud, with no excess oozing out.

MANY DRYWALL APPLICATIONS call for an adhesive in addition to screws or nails. Adhesives can be used to fasten drywall to another gypsum board, as well as to wood, masonry, or metal. Although they generally are not essential, adhesives can double a wall's tensile strength, increase its sheer strength by 50 percent, and dampen sound transmission. If you're applying panels over existing walls, adhesives can reduce the number of fasteners required by as much as 75 percent.

Application. Before you start, trim the adhesive tube to a diameter that will produce the proper size of bead. Apply the adhesive right to the face of the studs with a caulking gun. Run the adhesive bead to within 6 inches of the ends of each frame member. Fasten the drywall to the adhesive immediately, before it has a chance to set up (within about 15 minutes). Figure on using about four gallons of adhesive for every 1,000 square feet of drywall coverage.

Types. Use a stud adhesive (construction adhesive) in combination with nails or screws to attach drywall to wood or metal studs or directly to concrete or masonry. An ideal bead measures ¼ to ⅜ inch wide. Use a laminating adhesive between layers of drywall in double-layer applications, and also to attach drywall to concrete or rigid foam insulation (polystyrene or urethane). Apply a bead of adhesive at the location of each frame member when attaching the face layer in a multilayer application.

DRYWALL EDGES

THE MOST COMMON edge found on standard drywall panels is the **tapered edge.** On the face side of the panel (the side that faces the room), the long edges taper slightly to form a recess about 1/20 inch deep. This allows tape and joint compound to be applied flush with the face of the panel.

Square-edged drywall has edges identical in thickness to the body of the panel. With this material, all joints are similar to those created when you join regular panels end to end. With practice, you can finish adjoining square edges neatly with tape and joint compound. However, square-edged panels are best used where no finishing is required, as in the bottom layer of a two-layer application.

Tongue-and-groove drywall panels have interlocking V-shape edges. Finishing these edges takes serious skill, and tongue-and-groove stock is rarely used in applications that require finishing. The locking tongue and groove provides resistance against wind and water, which explains why tongue-and-groove panels are recommended for use under some exterior siding, stucco, and shingles.

Beveled edges, which you don't see that often, are meant to be left unfinished to give the room a paneled look. Unfortunately, in rooms that won't take all full panels, it's difficult to lay out the panels so that each joint will have two clean beveled edges.

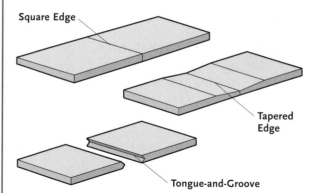

Square Edge

Tapered Edge

Tongue-and-Groove

Edge Treatments. The three most common edges: square edges (which create butt joints), tapered edges (ideal for drywall panels that will be finished with tape and joint compound), and tongue-and-groove (common with vapor-barrier-creating drywall panels).

DEALING WITH DRYWALL EDGES

Drywall edges and butt ends don't always meet in perfectly straight, tightly made seams that can be finished with tape and joint compound. Sometimes you need to fasten metal or plastic accessories to the panels (or to the framing beneath the panels)—for example, to help reinforce an outside corner or protect a joint where drywall abuts another surface.

L-bead allows a panel to abut a window or door casing. However, it is used with casings that aren't designed to cover the drywall's edge. L-bead creates a recess between the casing and the panel.

Bullnose corner bead and **flexible bead** are made of vinyl. Bullnose bead provides a rounded 90-degree corner for a "soft" appearance. Flexible bead is used in any joint that involves a curved outside corner, as in an archway or above a curved window. This L-shaped bead has one notched and one solid flange. As you apply the bead to the corner, the notches spread out to adjust for the curve, and you then screw through the flanges to hold the bead in place.

A product called **arch bead** is also available for finishing curved edges. Both the vinyl bead and the metal, V-shaped sides are flexible and can be pressed into any curved or irregular shape without having to be cut. Arch bead is available at many home centers.

Drywall clips are L-shaped pieces of metal or plastic, with each wing of the clip measuring about 2 inches wide. They are used most commonly to attach partition walls to floor and ceiling framing. You install these clips to provide a screwing base and backing on a drywall edge that doesn't face onto a stud or joist.

CORNER BEAD

CORNER BEAD is an L-shaped piece of galvanized steel with holes drilled in its flanges. This material reinforces the outside corner where two drywall panels meet. After you attach corner bead by clinching or by nailing or screwing through the drywall into the framing, you finish it using joint compound but no tape. When properly installed and finished, these steel angles strengthen the corner and define it with a clean straight line. The nose, or raised bead, also acts as a kind of screed guide for your knife when applying joint compound.

Corner Protection. Attach metal corner bead to outside corners with drywall nails about every 6 inches. The raised bead guides the drywall knife to create smooth finished edges for joint compound.

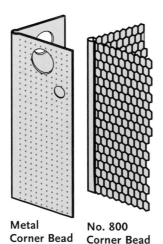

Metal
Corner Bead

No. 800
Corner Bead

J-BEAD

J-BEAD (ALSO CALLED J-TRIM) is used in places where a drywall panel abuts a brick wall, window jamb, shower stall, or other structure. To attach J-bead, you drive screws or nails through the face of the panel and the bead's back flange.

Finishing-type has a front flange that requires finishing with joint compound. Reveal-type J-bead, on the other hand, is not designed to be finished with joint compound. Because J-bead wraps snugly around the panel edge, it must be matched to the thickness of the gypsum drywall panel.

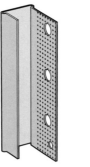  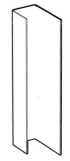

Metal J-Bead
(Finishing Type)

Metal J-Bead
(Reveal Type)

Plastic J-Bead
(Reveal Type)

Edge Treatment. J-bead is used where drywall abuts non-drywalled surfaces. Finishing type is finished with joint compound; reveal type is left unfinished.

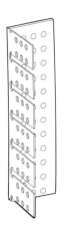

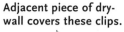
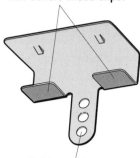

Metal
L-Bead

Plastic
L-Bead

Adjacent piece of dry-
wall covers these clips.

Nail this section
into stud or plate.

Another Edge Finish.
L-bead is installed where
drywall abuts a non-dry-
walled finished edge. The
flange on the face of the
drywall is finished with
joint compound.

Round Corner.
Bullnose corner
bead is a vinyl treat-
ment that provides
a soft 90° corner.
Finish it as you
would metal bead.

Arch Finish.
Flexible vinyl cor-
ner bead is used
to finish the joints
at the top of
arches and other
curved edges.

**Another Arch
Bead.** Wire arch
bead provides a
curved edge for
finishing with joint
compound. Use it
to finish arch tops.

Attachment Point.
Drywall clips provide
backing for drywall
edges that miss fram-
ing members. They
are attached to an ad-
jacent stud or plate.

FLEXIBLE METAL CORNER TAPE

FLEXIBLE METAL CORNER TAPE
typically measures 2 inches wide and
has two ½-inch-wide galvanized metal
strips running along each side of a
center crease. It is designed for use on
outside and inside corners that form an
angle greater than 90 degrees, replacing
corner bead. Install it with the metal
side facing inward, and apply joint compound as you would to conventional
paper tape.

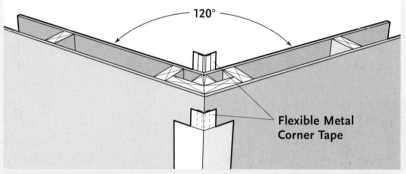

120°

Flexible Metal
Corner Tape

Flexible Metal Corner Tape. Used where the angle of an outside or
inside corner exceeds 90 degrees, this paper corner tape has metal
strips running down its center.

pro tip

WIRE SHIELDS, ALSO CALLED NAIL PLATES,
ARE SMALL 1½-INCH (STUD-WIDTH) BY 2-
INCH METAL PLATES WITH FOUR POINTED
LEGS THAT GET HAMMERED INTO THE STUD
FACES. INSTALL SHIELDS WHEREVER A FAS-
TENER MIGHT PROTRUDE INTO WIRING OR
PIPING RUNNING WITHIN A STUD.

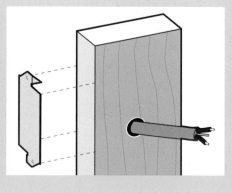

Wire Shields. These
metal plates should
be installed on the
face of a stud if there
is a risk of a screw or
nail penetrating pipes
or wiring running
within the stud wall.

TAPING MATERIALS

To finish seams and cover screw- or nailheads, you'll need to seal the panels' adjoining edges with drywall tape and apply various layers of joint compound. This part of the job will stand out most noticeably if you make a mistake. It takes a good eye and some skill to make joints that appear perfectly flat.

Finishing Materials. To complete your drywalling job, you'll need to apply drywall tape and joint compound. You can also finish the whole room with a texturing compound.

TAPE TYPES

DRYWALL TAPE, either fiberglass or paper, is used as a base for multiple layers of joint compound. For years, paper tape was the only product you could buy. Today, many professional drywallers (those who have lots of practice) use the more expensive self-sticking fiberglass tape (also called mesh) for many applications.

Fiberglass tape is a net-like mesh that comes in 1½- to 2-inch-wide rolls up to 300 feet long. You simply apply this self-sticking material to a dry seam and then follow it with multiple coats of joint compound.

Flexible corner tape is made of paper and thin metal. It is used on corners that vary from 90 degrees.

Paper tape measures 2 inches wide and comes in rolls up to 500 feet long. It has a crease down the center, which makes for easier folding on inside corner applications. If you're a beginning drywaller, you'll have an easier time with paper tape. It resists wrinkling better than fiberglass tape, and it trims more easily to the right length—just use the edge of your taping knife to cut it. Paper tape takes longer to apply than fiberglass tape, however, because you have to spread a base layer of joint compound before applying the tape to the seam.

Some manufacturers perforate paper tape with weep holes to allow joint compound to saturate it. Perforated tape costs a little more than the standard type, but it makes the job of bedding and covering the seams slightly easier.

Three Tapes. Fiberglass mesh drywall tape (left) is treated with a mild adhesive. The tape sticks in place along drywall seams and is then covered with three layers of joint compound. Flexible metal corner tape (center) is used on outside and inside corners greater or less than 90 degrees. Paper drywall tape (right) is embedded in a base coat of joint compound and then covered with two more coats of joint compound.

Joint Compounds and Textures

Joint compound, sometimes called mud, comes in two general formulas, each of which includes several types that have specific applications. The two general formulas are vinyl-based drying-type compound, which hardens as the water medium dries, and setting-type compound, which is hardened by a chemical reaction that is catalyzed by water.

Drying-type compound is sold in both powdered and premixed form. The latter, which comes in 1-, 2½-, and 5-gallon buckets, is more commonly used today. Of the three basic types of this formula, taping compound is applied first to adhere the tape to the drywall seam. Topping compound is used for both the middle coat (often called the filler coat) and for the finish coat. The third type, all-purpose compound, is used for all three coats and is by far the most popular.

No matter which variety of premixed drying-type compound you use, always start with fresh product, and seal the container securely between applications. (When you've emptied a bucket of joint compound, clean it out with water and keep it within reach. These buckets make excellent stepstools and catchalls.)

Setting-type compound comes only in powdered form. Because these products set faster and harder than drying-type compounds and better resist cracking, they are generally preferred by professionals who want to work quickly. With this type of compound, you can apply consecutive coats to the drywall in the same day. Setting time varies from ½ to 6 hours. This type also resists sanding more than drying-type compounds, so it pays to get a nice finish, or polish, during the application rather than depending on sanding.

Special fire-resistant joint compounds are also available (with trade names such as Fire Shield and Fire-Halt). These compounds provide fire resistance and help to prevent fires from spreading through joints in walls and ceilings.

ESTIMATING MATERIAL

QUALITY DRYWALLING REQUIRES accurate estimates of material quantities. Nothing breaks your stride like having to run out to the store for materials once you've started a job. Here are some tips on how to estimate materials.

- **Joint Compound:** You'll need roughly a gallon for every 100 square feet of gypsum drywall.
- **Joint Tape:** To finish 500 square feet of drywall, figure on using 400 feet of tape.
- **Nails/Screws:** This figure can vary depending on stud spacing (walls framed 16 inches on center require more fasteners than those framed at 24 inches) and on your nail or screw schedule (panels attached with adhesive require fewer fasteners). Figure on one fastener for every square foot of drywall in your job. For example, an 18 x 18-foot ceiling (324 square feet) will require about 320 screws or nails. Because one pound of 1-inch drywall screws contains about 320 screws, you'll need a pound of screws for every 320 square feet of drywall.
- **Drywall Panels:** Estimating how much drywall you'll need to cover a room is a matter of square footage. Calculate the wall surface of the room, and divide that figure by the square footage of the panels you intend to use. For instance, a 4 x 8-foot panel measures 32 square feet. If you have a 1,000-square-foot room, you'll need just over 31 panels. Because they come in units of two, order 32 panels. When estimating square footage, don't subtract the door or window areas (except for bay windows or unusually large doors), because you'll need extra for mistakes.

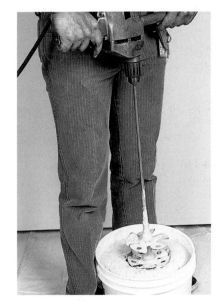

Preparing the Compound. All joint compounds, even the premixed types, need to be stirred before use. A well-mixed compound will go on smoothly with fewer bubbles. Mixing also ensures that the product has consistent water content.

The best accessory for mixing joint compound is a heavy-duty drill loaded with a mixing paddle. If you prefer to mix by hand (which is better for premixed joint compound), use a potato-masher-type hand mixer on a 2-foot handle. If the product is too stiff, add small amounts of water and agitate.

FINISHING WALL PANELS

Drywall panels are never left exposed in living areas, but not all drywall jobs require the same type of finishing—the level of drywall finish needed for a tile wall differs from the level required for a high-gloss paint finish, for example. What's best for your job? Professionals have been arguing about the proper level of finish for some time. To reach a conclusion that everyone can agree upon, four trade associations—the Gypsum Association, the Painting and Decorating Contractors of America, the Association of the Walls and Ceiling Industries International, and the Ceiling Interior Systems Construction Association—developed a consensus document called, "Recommended Levels of Gypsum Board Finish." This document spells out taping and joint compound requirements based on how the panels will be decorated. (See "Recommended Levels of Drywall Finish," page 162.)

Easy Plastering. New simpler-to-use plaster systems provide the looks and durability of traditional plaster systems.

Finish Treatments. The final finish you select will determine the level of drywall treatment.

Spray-on Primers. New primers can provide a skim-coated-type surface for paints.

Typical Finishes

For the majority of drywall jobs, most drywallers cover the installed panels with a high-grade primer/sealer. This provides a base for finish coats of paint, and it prevents the porous panels from absorbing the top coats of paint. For high-gloss painted finishes or finishes that will be under intensive light, many professionals finish the panels with a skim coat of drywall compound before applying the primer and paint.

Special Finishes. With the popularity of decorative paint techniques and the use of glossier paint sheens on walls and ceilings, manufacturers have introduced a variety of finish products. For example, new primers developed in conjunction with drywall manufacturers provide the same finishing opportunities as a skim-coated wall. These products are designed for use in high-light areas under glossy finishes.

A number of plaster-type products provide the smoothness and durability of traditional plaster walls. The systems come in one- and two-coat varieties that expand the decorating potential of a typical drywall system. Be sure to check with the finish manufacturer to make sure the plaster-type product is compatible with the drywall panels you plan on installing.

DRYWALL SUSPENSION SYSTEMS

PRE-ENGINEERED SYSTEMS make installing suspended ceilings simpler than ever. Suspended ceilings are a good choice when you want to install new drywall over an old ceiling that is not level.

Using suspended ceiling technology, some systems go beyond flat ceilings, allowing for the construction of domes, ceiling vaults, and decorative soffits, opening up a range of decorative looks that was once reserved for custom-built homes or commercial buildings. Suspended ceiling systems save time and money. Interlocking components arrive on the job site ready to be fitted together. On-site fabrication of steel channels is minimal. With the exception of flat suspended ceilings, most of the newer ceiling systems are best left to professionals. Many are custom-built based on an architect's plans. (For more information see, "Suspended Ceilings," page 60.)

Domes, Arches, Deep Soffits. New suspended ceiling systems enable a range of decorative possibilities.

2 tools & equipment

ANY DRYWALL JOB, large or small, requires four kinds of tools and equipment: safety equipment to protect eyes and lungs; marking and cutting instruments that ensure precise lengths, angles, and holes; hanging tools to position and fasten panels; and finishing equipment to apply joint compound and sand seams.

THE RIGHT STUFF

As with other facets of residential construction, the tools and equipment for drywalling have improved over the years. Panel jacks make hanging ceilings easier by eliminating the need to balance panels on your head. Strap-on stilts can save a thousand ladder or scaffold moves. A tape bender and cornering tools can save hours of sanding corner seams, and modern dust barriers help contain a job's mess. You may not need every tool and accessory described in this chapter for every job, but it helps to know the available options before you dive into your next project.

PERSONAL SAFETY EQUIPMENT

GYPSUM DRYWALL and the products used to install and finish it generally contain no toxic substances. However, the dominant byproduct of installation, referred to by NIOSH and OSHA as *nuisance dust*, will irritate your eyes and lungs. To save yourself unnecessary aggravation, wear protective gear, especially when sawing and sanding.

Dust Mask. Important when cutting drywall and sanding joints, a dust mask protects the lungs from the irritating dust created by powdered gypsum and joint compound.

Dust-Mist Respirator. You can buy changeable filters for a respirator if you're particularly sensitive to dust.

Safety Glasses. Eye protection is recommended when installing drywall, especially when working on a ceiling. Chunks of crumbling drywall and dust can fall into your eyes, causing severe irritation and possibly permanent damage.

Lower-Back Support. This harness is desirable when lifting and manipulating drywall panels, which can weigh 45 to 70 lbs. each.

Hardhat. This can be useful to protect your head while holding up ceiling panels—provided you add a sponge on top to protect the panel.

Panel Carrier. One person can easily carry 8-ft. drywall panels by hooking a carrier onto one edge of the panel. To prevent back injury, avoid quick movements as you rise to a standing position.

MEASURING & MARKING TOOLS

A QUALITY JOB begins with accurately measuring and marking drywall panels to make clean, crisp cuts. Invest in a good-quality 25-foot measuring tape; you will reach for it dozens of times when working with drywall. Use a chalk-line box and T-square when straight cuts are in order. For butting panels against a masonry wall, scribe the edges of the panel using a compass.

Claw Hammer. This common tool is good to have for quick framing changes and alterations.

Chalk-Line Box. This tool is handy when cutting long lengths of drywall panels. "Snapping a line" is often the only way to get a long, clean, straight cut line.

Screwdrivers. Phillips-head and flat-blade screwdrivers are essential for simple mechanical and electrical repairs and adjustments.

Accurate Measurements. A sturdy 25-ft. measuring tape is the most basic drywalling tool you'll use.

Finding Studs. An electronic stud finder lets you find and mark the locations of wall studs easily and quickly.

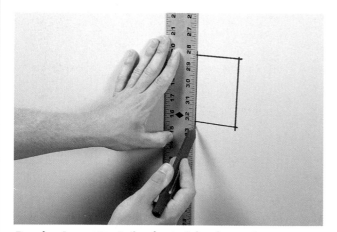

Precise Layouts. A simple straightedge and a carpenter's pencil helps you lay out drywall cuts with precision.

One-Shot Cut Lines. A 4-foot aluminum T-square lets you draw square lines across the width of an entire panel.

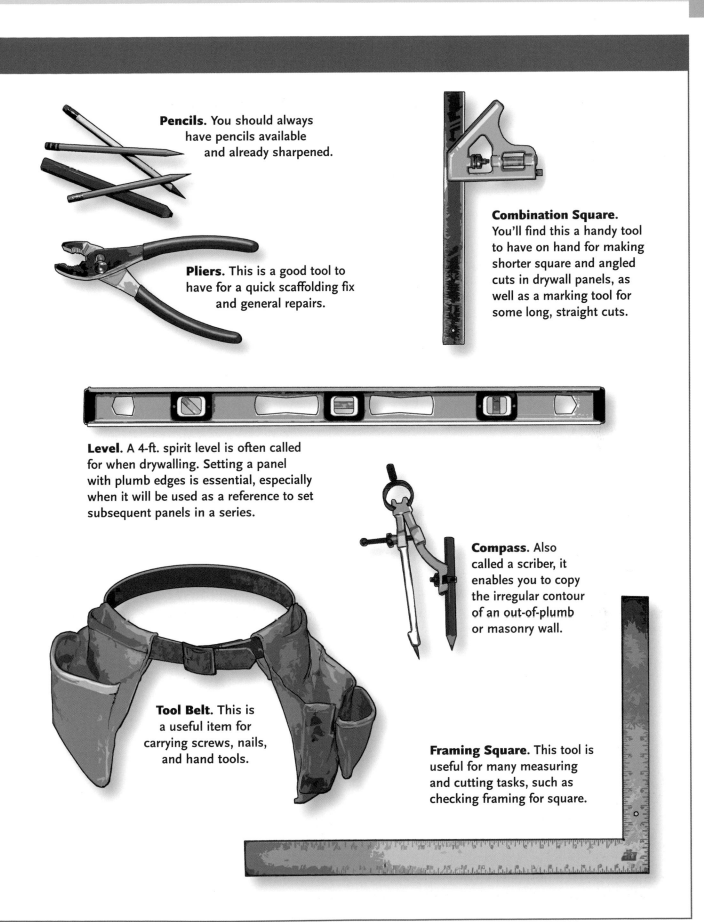

Pencils. You should always have pencils available and already sharpened.

Combination Square. You'll find this a handy tool to have on hand for making shorter square and angled cuts in drywall panels, as well as a marking tool for some long, straight cuts.

Pliers. This is a good tool to have for a quick scaffolding fix and general repairs.

Level. A 4-ft. spirit level is often called for when drywalling. Setting a panel with plumb edges is essential, especially when it will be used as a reference to set subsequent panels in a series.

Compass. Also called a scriber, it enables you to copy the irregular contour of an out-of-plumb or masonry wall.

Tool Belt. This is a useful item for carrying screws, nails, and hand tools.

Framing Square. This tool is useful for many measuring and cutting tasks, such as checking framing for square.

HANGING & CUTTING TOOLS

MOST DRYWALL JOBS require only a few simple tools to obtain pro-quality results. You can make straight cuts using a simple utility knife fitted with a sharp blade and a utility saw to make cutouts for electrical receptacle boxes. A drywall hammer does a better job than a standard claw hammer. Or use a cordless drill-driver for driving drywall screws. There are for speciality cutting projects.

Drywall Hammer. This special hammer is designed to drive nails and leave a dimple around the nailhead. The hammer has a symmetrical convex face for this purpose. The dull tapered blade is for levering and fine-tuning panel position.

Drywall Ripper. This tool has two opposing blades that spin around a pin-pointed center axis. This tool is handy for trimming strips less than 5 in. wide.

Utility Knife. This is the tool most often used to cut drywall panels. Be sure it is loaded with a fresh, sharp razor blade, or it will tear the face paper as it cuts. Keep a supply of replacement blades handy.

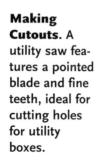

Making Cutouts. A utility saw features a pointed blade and fine teeth, ideal for cutting holes for utility boxes.

For Driving Screws. A cordless drill that feature an adjustable clutch ensures consistent screwhead depth.

Applying Adhesive. A caulking gun is a necessary tool if you plan to attach your panels with adhesive.

Lifting Panels. A panel lifter, which resembles a miniature seesaw, makes it easy to lift a drywall panel 2 or 3 inches.

Drywall Saw. This saw is good for cutting out door and window openings and trimming excess.

Drywalling Screw Gun. Load a screw into the bit of this special tool, designed just for driving drywall screws. When the screw is driven to the proper depth, a clutch will disengage the bit, leaving the screw just below the surface of the drywall's face.

Power Cutting Tool. A cutout tool can save a lot of time making holes, but it also raises a lot of dust. Pros generally use this tool to cut around electrical outlets and fixtures, such as recessed lighting.

Surface-Forming Rasp. Use this device to shave off small amounts of drywall along the edges of the panels. It's a handy tool to have if you have cut your drywall panel just a hair too long.

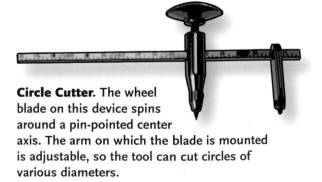

Circle Cutter. The wheel blade on this device spins around a pin-pointed center axis. The arm on which the blade is mounted is adjustable, so the tool can cut circles of various diameters.

Aviation Snips. A high-quality pair of snips is needed to cut various metal and plastic corner beads and edgings to size.

FINISHING TOOLS

THE RIGHT TOOLS can help you obtain a smooth final finish. Fill drywall joints with drywall joint compound; smooth the compound using a number of knives that get wider as you proceed through the job. Sand the joint compound between coats to achieve a professional-quality, seamless finish.

2- to 3-in. Knife. These small knives are the tools for applying joint compound in tight spaces, like the area between a corner door frame and a wall, where larger knives won't fit.

Taping Knives. The 6-in. taping knife will be in your hand more than any other drywall tool—spend a little more to get the highest quality.

5- or 6-in. Knife. This is the tool that gets the most use on all drywall jobs. It is great for applying joint compound and for scooping fresh joint compound out of a bucket.

Two-Faced Corner Knife. This knife can help leave a professional finish on joint compound in corners, though it takes practice to master.

12-in. Straight-Handled Knife. This drywall knife is required for applying wider coats of joint compound. Having one on site is an absolute must.

12- to 16-in. Finishing Trowel. Use this trowel to smooth coats of joint compound. Its long blade enables you to leave a wide, consistent finish while keeping blade marks to a minimum.

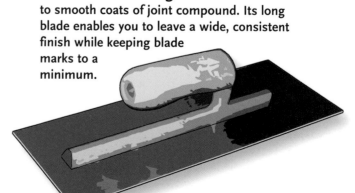

Mud Trays. Trays such as these, which can be held in one hand, allow you to carry small amounts of compound with you as you finish a room.

Hawk. A hawk allows you to carry wet joint compound with you as you finish joints and fastener-head voids.

Hand Sander. This is a practical, easy way to sand walls and ceilings. Load it with half sheets of 120-grit sandpaper.

Sanding Pole. A long pole with a universal joint is a convenient and simple way to sand walls and ceilings. Load it with 120-grit sandpaper.

Tape Dispenser. Hung from your belt, this is a convenient way to dispense paper tape while working.

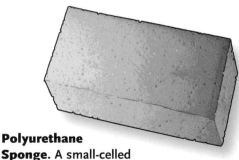

Polyurethane Sponge. A small-celled sponge offers a dust-free alternative to sanding. It is ideal in areas that can tolerate no dust, like an office or a finished area that requires only a single wall or patch installed.

GAINING EXTRA HEIGHT

SHOE STILTS strap onto your shoes and calves, giving you an extra 18 to 24 inches of height and thereby eliminating the need for scaffolding or ladders. They save a great deal of time and effort, but can be difficult to use and are not permitted by all safety codes.

Scaffolding. On most drywall jobs, you will need to place drywall panels with the aid of a ladder, bench, or scaffold—something to provide you and your helper with the extra height to reach the work area. Stepladders work well enough for small jobs, but if you are drywalling an entire room, the act of installing a panel and then moving two ladders so that you and a helper can lift the next panel into position will slow you down. For large jobs, consider using a rolling scaffold. The scaffold allows you to work at a comfortable height and is easy to move. Working on a scaffold is safer than trying to keep your balance on a step-ladder, especially when holding a drywall panel.

Pros own their own scaffolds, but you can rent one from a tool rental shop.

A **panel jack** or panel lift can save a lot of back-breaking work during ceiling installation, especially if you're working alone. An adjustable metal frame that cradles the panel can be raised or lowered by cranking a handle. The entire jack is mounted on casters and maneuvers easily. Raise the panel into place, and the panel jack holds it snugly until you've secured it. This device also works well for mounting panels high on tall walls.

A **deadman,** also called a T-brace or T-support, is a handy accessory you can make yourself. (See opposite.) You wedge the deadman beneath a ceiling panel, pinning it in place for screwing or nailing. The top piece of the deadman should be covered with a piece of foam or scrap of carpet to protect the ceiling from damage.

Shoe Stilts. You can gain up to 2 feet of height by strapping these onto your shoes; however, using them takes practice and they are not permitted by all safety codes.

Scaffold. Consider using a rolling scaffold for larger jobs. It will allow you to work at a comfortable height and is easy to move.

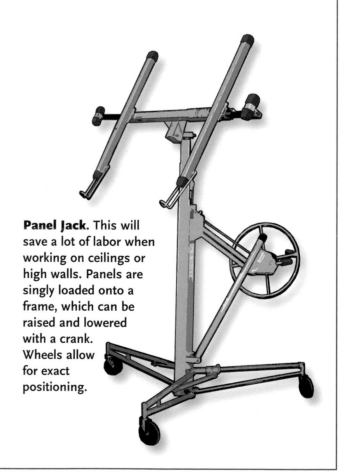

Panel Jack. This will save a lot of labor when working on ceilings or high walls. Panels are singly loaded onto a frame, which can be raised and lowered with a crank. Wheels allow for exact positioning.

BUILDING A DEADMAN

A DEADMAN IS A BRACE that allows you to install ceiling panels while working alone. This site-built tool is made using 2×4s that are fashioned into a reinforced T-shape. The overall height of the deadman should be high enough to allow you to wedge the deadman under the ceiling panel. However, if the fit is too tight, you many damage the panel. Another option is to build the deadman about 2 inches short of the actual ceiling height. At that height, the panel will rest just below the ceiling joists when you lift it into position, allowing you to push the panel into place against the joist with one hand while you attach the panel with the other hand.

Make the crosspiece about 3 feet long to provide adequate support across the width of the panels. To protect the drywall, attach scrap carpeting or foam to the top of the crosspiece. Add reinforcement by nailing angle braces as shown below. It is also a good idea to attach a section of rubber hose to the bottom of the vertical support to keep the deadman from slipping on the floor.

To use the deadman, attach a temporary nailer to support one end of the sheet. Lift the sheet into position, and apply pressure with the deadman. Be sure to keep the crosspiece under a ceiling joist. Don't apply pressure to an unsupported section of drywall.

1 Build a basic T-shape support out of 2x4s. Overall height should be about 2 in. short of the ceiling.

2 Keep the main support from wobbling by attaching angle braces of 2x4s or lighter wood.

3 A temporary nailer supports one end of the sheet while you raise the other with the deadman.

4 Keep applying pressure to the deadman to prevent the panel from slipping off the nailer.

KEEPING THE WORKSITE CLEAN

DRYWALLING CREATES DUST. Even if you use a dust-free sanding method (such as a dampened sanding sponge), cutting and installing the panels is dusty work. Dust will drift invisibly through open doorways, or even underneath a closed door, and will settle on every surface in your home. You'll need a dust curtain over each doorway or wall area that opens into an occupied room and floor protection for any finished area that you are likely to traverse. You should also vacuum the site at the end of each work day.

There is some fairly sophisticated dust-control equipment available, but you can make your own by using furring strips, duct tape, and 6-mil polyethylene plastic (the kind sold as painter's dropcloth). Trap a sheet of plastic against an unfinished wall over a door opening with furring strips, and then screw through the furring and plastic sheet into the wall. If you will need to use a doorway, slit the plastic wall down the center, and drape a wide plastic curtain over the slit.

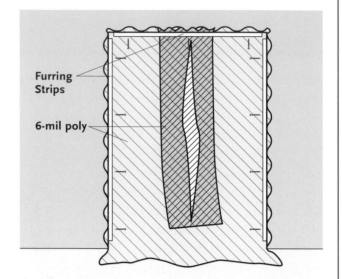

Furring Strips

6-mil poly

Dust Barrier. Although you can buy commercial barriers with zippers, you can also make one using furring and 6-mil polyethylene. Tack a piece of plastic in a doorway, and slit an opening in its center. Drape another piece over it, which will act as a door.

ELECTRICAL BOX EXTENDERS

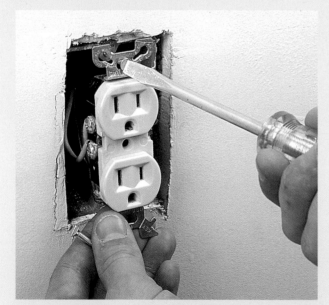

1 Bring existing switch and outlet boxes flush with new drywall by adding extensions. Start by turning off the power and removing the device.

2 Add a code-approved extension to the existing box; screw the outlet or switch back in place; and turn on the power. Then add the new layer of drywall.

Tools & Equipment

MECHANICAL FINISHING TOOLS

MECHANICAL TOOLS can speed the taping and finishing process. Most tool sets contain a basic applicator with interchangeable heads to complete different phases of the taping process.

The basic taping tool applies the tape and a thin layer of joint compound in one pass. Most are designed to completely fill the tapered seam between drywall panels. Other tools apply wider layers of compound to complete the seam taping process just as you would when finishing by hand. There are also tools to tape and apply joint compound to inside and outside corners, and special heads to fill fastener indentations.

With some models, joint compound is loaded into the tool and then squeezed out during application. Other tools are pneumatically driven, using air to pump joint compound from a reservoir. Better types of tools allow you to adjust the flow rate so that you can apply joint compound to suit your needs.

Mechanical tools have a number of advantages over hand taping. Once you have mastered the tools, you will find you achieve consistent results. The work will go quicker and there will be less sanding at the end of the project. The downside to automatic tools is that they are expensive. Unless you plan on drywalling an entire house, it is probably best to stick with hand tools. Mechanical applicators also take some time to learn how to use correctly.

Some professionals send their crews to classes conducted by the tool manufacturer. To keep the tools operating effectively, you will need to closely follow instructions for cleanup. And even if you do use mechanical tapers, most drywall jobs will still require some hand finishing.

Finishing Corners. This tool contains small tabs that convert a coater to a tool for finishing corner bead.

Angled Heads. Mechanical tapers with angled heads allow you to complete vertical seams easily.

Tapered Seams. By switching coater heads you can apply wider layers of joint compound to finish tapered seams.

3 preparing to drywall

YOU CAN'T OVERSTATE THE IMPORTANCE of carefully preparing a wall or ceiling

for drywalling. Because the panels measure only ½ inch or so thick, they roughly contour

the framing members or other surface to which they're fastened. Any irregularity, such as

an out-of-plumb-on-the-face or protruding stud or joist, will show through the drywall

panel once it's up. To prevent unpleasant surprises, you need to know how to locate and

correct these irregularities before they compromise your drywalling job.

CREATING LAYOUTS

Before preparing the walls and ceilings, you'll want to create a layout plan that uses as many full panels (4 × 8 feet or longer) as possible. Fewer joints make for less mess, less waste, and less taping work (which accounts for most of the man-hours in any drywalling project). This chapter will offer some strategies for reducing panel usage and a few common framing practices that make it easier to use your materials to the best advantage.

Getting the Most Out of Your Materials

The following schematics show typical horizontal installations for 10-, 16-, and 20-foot-long walls. Notice in each case that a bit of planning can reduce the number of panels required and the occurrence of end-butted joints. Note also how the various layouts affect the linear footage of joints that need finishing.

LAYING OUT A DRYWALL JOB

DRYWALLING MAY WELL RANK FIRST among the most wasteful of the construction trades, partly because the material is relatively inexpensive. Trimming a 4 × 8-foot panel to fit a 3 × 6-foot space leaves you with odd-shaped cutoffs that can't be used elsewhere. Ideally, you would install a single piece of custom-fitted drywall large enough to cover an entire wall. Because that's impossible in most cases, you go with the largest pieces you can handle. This invariably means cutting large sheets down to size—you never want to patch together smaller pieces to fill out a wall. If some waste occurs along the way (and it will), that's the price of doing a clean, professional job.

Keep in mind the following three objectives when laying out any drywall job:

- Minimize the number of joints by using the smallest number of the largest panels that fit in your room.
- Avoid end-butted flush joints, which usually require joining two untapered panel ends.
- Set up the layout for ease of installation by eliminating multiple moves of wallboard stacks, ladders, scaffolding, and so on.

THE 10-FOOT WALL

OF THE TWO LAYOUTS shown below, one uses three 4 x 8-foot panels and one uses two 4 x 10-foot panels but requires no cutting.

Layout Number 1 uses three 4 × 8-foot panels rather inefficiently on this 10 x 8-foot wall. The resulting installation leaves you with a 2 × 8-foot cutoff, which creates a long end-butted flush joint—a difficult type of joint to tape. In total, you end up with a total of 16 linear feet of joint to tape and finish. Using longer panels solves these problems.

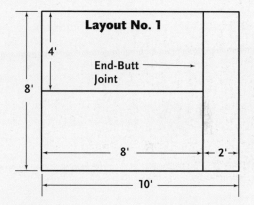

Layout Number 2 shows two 4 × 10-foot panels installed horizontally on the 10 x 8-foot wall. This, the recommended installation, is by far the more efficient way to install the panels on this size wall. This layout yields no cutoffs, no end-butted flush joint, and only 10 linear feet of taping and finishing work. And there is no waste material.

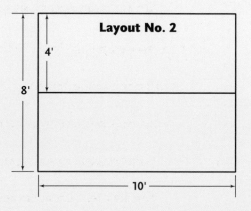

THE 16-FOOT WALL

OF THE FOUR ALTERNATIVES presented here on this 16 x 8-foot wall, only numbers 2 and 4 eliminate end-butt flush joints, and of those two, the fourth (and recommended) installation leaves fewer linear feet of finish work.

Layout Number 1 shows two 4 × 12-foot panels installed horizontally, with an 8-foot-long panel installed vertically at one end. While you won't need to cut any panels for this layout, it does leave you with 20 linear feet of joint to finish, including an end-butt joint that runs from floor to ceiling.

Layout Number 2 uses four 8-foot panels installed vertically. This eliminates end-butt joints, but you have 24 linear feet of joint to finish, which many consider a good tradeoff. Although it is a good alternative to "Layout Number 1," it is not the optimal design. Note that vertical seams are more difficult to finish than horizontal joints.

Layout Number 3 is a variation of the above layout. You will still install four panels, and you won't need to cut the panels. But this design yields a long end-butt joint to finish. The end-butt joint runs from floor to ceiling and is located right in the middle of the wall, where it will draw attention to itself. You also end up with 24 linear feet of joint overall to finish.

Layout Number 4, the recommended one, calls for just two 4 × 16-foot panels. This installation leaves you with no wasted wallboard, no end-butt flush joints, and just 16 linear feet of taping and finishing work along the horizontal seam. If you have a project similar to this one, make every effort to locate 16-foot-long panels.

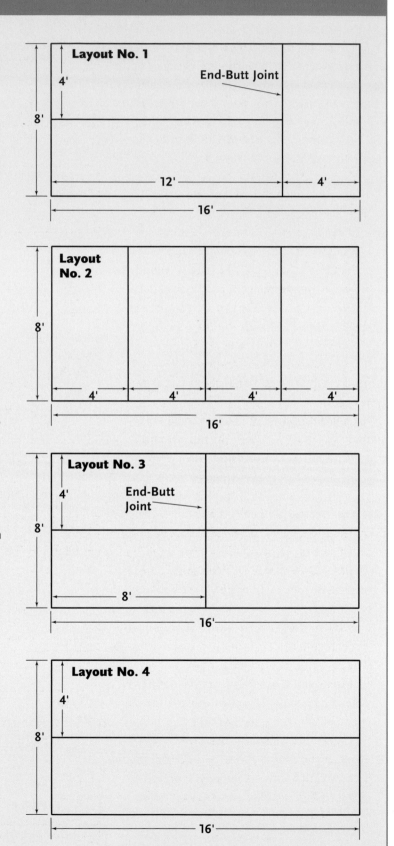

THE 20-FOOT WALL

OF THE FIVE LAYOUTS shown here, one eliminates end-butt joints and one places short-end butt joints near either end of the wall in staggered fashion, which makes them less noticeable. Both are recommended because they present tradeoffs between end-butt joints and longer tapered joints.

Layout Number 1 shows four 8-foot and two 4-foot panels installed horizontally. This installation yields two end-butt flush joints and a total of 36 linear feet of joint to finish. Although it creates no waste, it requires you to handle six individual pieces of drywall.

In Layout Number 2, four 10-foot-long panels create an end-butt joint in the most noticeable location—dead-center on the wall, running from floor to ceiling. This leaves you with only 28 linear feet of joint to finish, but the unfortunate placement of the end-butt joint outweighs this advantage.

Layout Number 3 calls for just three panels and yields a mere 24 linear feet of finishing work. Unfortunately, you end up with an obvious floor-to-ceiling end-butt joint.

In Layout Number 4, a recommended installation, you use a pair of 16-foot panels plus two 4-foot pieces to fill in the remaining areas. This solution avoids the continuous floor-to-ceiling end-butt joint by staggering the two long panels. You still have two 4-foot end-butt joints to finish, but this layout places them near each end of the wall, where they attract less attention. Overall, this installation requires just 28 linear feet of finish work, a substantial improvement over the 36 linear feet of layout number 1.

Layout Number 5 shows five 8-foot panels installed vertically with no end-butt joints, which is why it is recommended. However, this layout leaves you with 32 feet of joint to finish.

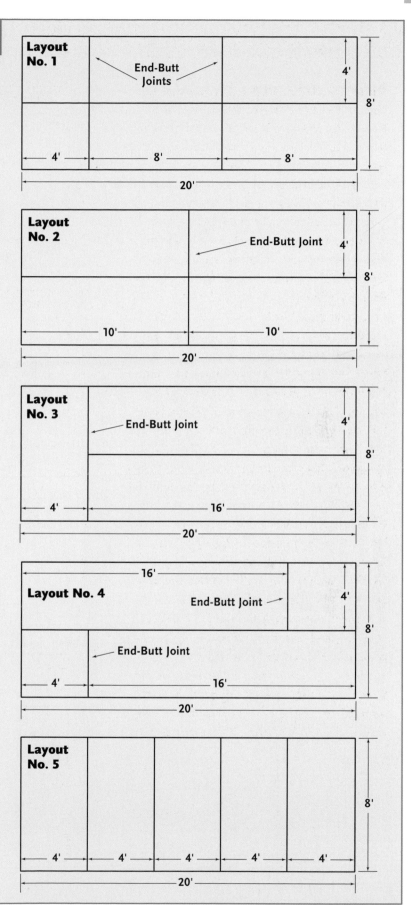

FRAMING DIMENSIONS AND DRYWALL

DRYWALL COMES IN A STANDARD 48-inch width because most framing codes require either a 16- or 24-inch on-center framing schedule. Whichever schedule is used, a 48-inch-wide panel installed parallel with studs or joists should end centered on a framing member.

It's critical that you work with accurately framed studs and joists. Each pair of adjoining panels must normally share a two-by that measures only 1½ inches wide, so accuracy is important. Note how on 16 inch on-center spacing two studs support the interior of the panel, while only one stud supports the interior on 24 inch on-center spacing.

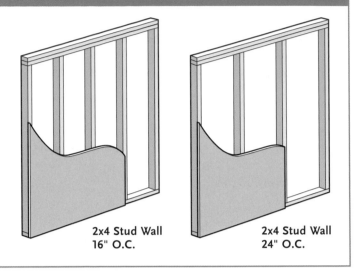

2x4 Stud Wall
16" O.C.

2x4 Stud Wall
24" O.C.

Framing Tips for Drywall. Check—and mark—joists and studs to be sure all panels have sufficient bearing. Also check for crooked, misaligned, or loose studs before you begin drywalling.

INSTALLING NAILER BLOCKS

BUILDERS OFTEN INSTALL top wall plates (the horizontal 2×4s or 2×6s that cap stud-framed walls) directly under ceiling joists. This can lead to problems later because it provides no fastening base for the edge of ceiling drywall. Without backing, the panel edge joint can crack over time. To add a fastening base, install blocking (the nailer block) that runs the full length of the top plate and extends half of its width beyond the top plate's inside edge.

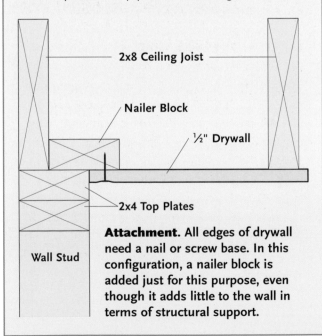

2x8 Ceiling Joist

Nailer Block

½" Drywall

2x4 Top Plates

Wall Stud

Attachment. All edges of drywall need a nail or screw base. In this configuration, a nailer block is added just for this purpose, even though it adds little to the wall in terms of structural support.

BACKING JOINTS AND EDGES

OPTIMALLY, panel edges should be fastened flush against framing members, whether they be furring strips, pieces of blocking, studs, or top/bottom plates. However, in some situations—for example, where drywall is installed horizontally on stud-framed walls or ceiling joists—nonbacked edges will bridge stud or joist bays. In these cases, you'll want 16-inch-on-center framing in order to reduce as much as possible the span between studs.

Of course, a remodeling job gives you no control over the existing framing, and you may be forced to drywall over 24-inch-on-center studs. If this is the case, and you're installing thinner (⅜-inch) panels, you'll need to install horizontal blocking between the stud bays. If you can't install blocking, either orient the drywall vertically or use thicker panels.

When installing full-length panels, you may be tempted to position two flush ends so that they meet in the middle of a stud bay. However, this would leave the end-butt joint unbacked, making it vulnerable to any slight pressure. To save yourself messy repair work later on, always back joints with a stud or furring strip, even though this often requires trimming the panel to

length. The same holds true for tapered edges. These long edges should always rest flush against, and be fastened to, some part of the framing, either furring strips, studs, or top plates.

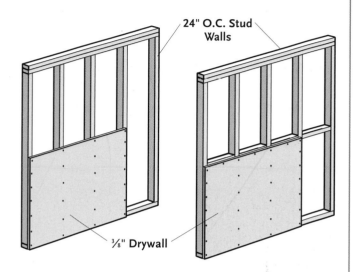

Backing. When hanging thin (⅜-in. or less) drywall horizontally, one edge of the panel may not have backing between studs (left). This could lead to cracking over time. In this situation, blocking should be added in each stud bay to accommodate the thinner panels (right).

STAGGERING END-BUTT JOINTS

IN MANY DRYWALL JOBS, you can't avoid creating end-butted joints (between untapered panel ends). This is especially true in long runs on walls or ceilings. Because end-butt joints make for difficult finish work and tend to draw attention to themselves (even when neatly finished), it's best not to align them on adjacent rows of drywall. If you must have end-butt joints, try to place them opposite each other near the ends of a wall. On ceilings or walls with long runs, start your first row of drywall with a half panel, the second row with a full panel, and so on, much the way a house is stagger-sheathed with plywood.

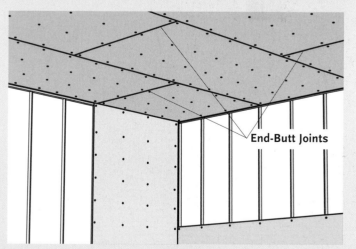

Stagger Joints. When installing panels on a wall or ceiling, stagger the end-butt flush joints as shown here. When end-butt seams are lined up, they call attention to themselves.

CORRECTING FRAMING MISTAKES

With today's declining lumber quality, more and more studs are bowed, cupped, or twisted. This can create problems for the drywaller, who depends on precise, predictable spacing between studs. In addition, every piece of framing should lie in the same plane so that drywall panels will hang perfectly flat. Inconsistency in the framing caused by bowed studs and misalignment will be broadcast through the drywall as wavy walls or bulges. So make sure all framing is alinged before installing drywall.

If part of a built-up ceiling beam or corner post protrudes, the panel must ride over this obstruction and will likely crack when you nail it home from the other side. If you can't pound down the obstruction with a framing hammer, use a surface-forming rasp to carve a shallow seat for the obstruction in the back of the drywall.

Check the Alignment. Examine the framing because drywall reflects any flaws in the supporting framing.

Detecting a Misaligned Stud

Difficulty Level: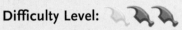

TOOLS & MATERIALS
▌ Measuring tape
▌ Three identical standoff blocks
▌ Hammer or cordless screw gun
▌ Three 10d nails or drywall screws
▌ Sturdy string as long as the wall

1 Install blocks. Attach one block at each end of the stud wall. Also partially attach a fastener, such as a nail, to the side of the block. The blocks should be at the same height.

2 Tie on string. Tie a string to the fasteners so that it stands off the stud wall a distance equal to the depth of the blocks.

3 Check for level plane. Try to slide the third block beneath the string. If studs are bowed outward, the string will impede the block, and you'll have to stretch the string to get it around the block. If studs are bowed inward, there will be a space between the block and the string. Check every stud in your wall.

4 Check on-center stud spacing. Use a measuring tape to make sure that the on-center spacing is consistent from stud to stud. Keep in mind that some studs must provide anchorage for two panels, so the on-center distance should come close to the center of those studs, no more than ¼ inch out of alignment. Correct a misplaced stud by withdrawing the nails, repositioning the stud, and renailing it in its proper location.

1 Check to see if a wall is straight by using the string-and-block standoff method. Use three blocks of the same size. Set one on each end of the wall with a string between them.

2 Tie off the string at one end as shown above. Pulling the string taut, loop the string several times around the other screw, inset. This will capture the string and keep it from slipping.

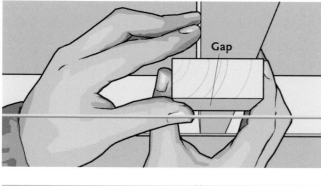

Gap

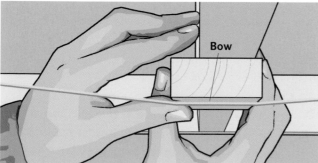

Bow

3 The gap or the bow between the string and the block will demonstrate the relationship of the stud to the rest of the wall.

4 Before drywalling, check to make sure the on-center distance between studs is consistent. Once the drywall is in place and hiding the studs, you will use the on-center spacing to guide the placement of fasteners.

47

Straightening a Stud

Difficulty Level:

TOOLS & MATERIALS
▌ Handsaw or circular saw
▌ 4-foot level
▌ 8-foot 2x6
▌ 12- to 24-inch pipe or bar clamp
▌ 2-foot-long scab boards to match your framing
▌ Hammer or screw gun
▌ 10d nails or 2½-inch screws

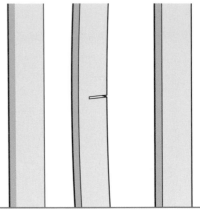

1 To straighten a bowed stud, cut a kerf with a handsaw or circular saw at the center of the bow on the concave edge.

Studs that are only slightly misaligned (¼ inch or so) because of a framing error can often be repositioned with a whack from a heavy framing hammer. Toenailing a couple of nails can sometimes pull a straight piece into place. If studs are straight and measure less than ¼ inch out of alignment, leave them alone. However, defective studs may have to be straightened or even replaced if they bulge out into the plane on which you intend to fasten drywall.

2 Attach a 2x6 across several studs on the side you have kerfed, and then fasten a clamp around the stud and the 2x6.

1 **Cut kerfs.** Using a handsaw or a circular saw (being careful to avoid kickback), cut a 1-inch-deep kerf into the concave edge of each stud that is bowing outward.

2 **Attach a board and clamp it.** Fasten a 2×6 board across several studs on the side you have kerfed. Then attach a clamp between the other side of the curved stud and the board, as shown in the illustration.

3 **Straighten and stabilize the stud.** Tighten the clamp: the kerf will open up, and the concave side of the stud will come even with the 2×6. Nail or screw on a scab board to the side of the stud to keep it straight. Then remove the clamp and the 2×6.

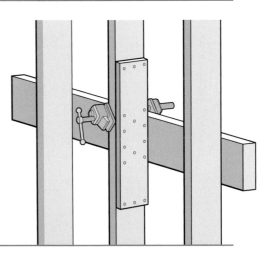

3 Tighten the clamp until the stud is flush with the board. Then attach a scab to the stud, and remove the clamp and board.

THE WEDGE METHOD

No. 1   No. 2   No. 3   No. 4

AN ALTERNATIVE METHOD is shown here. Kerf the concave side of the stud (No.2). Then drive a wooden wedge into the kerf with a hammer as you pull the stud toward you to open up the kerf (No.3) . The wedge will force apart the kerf. When the stud is straight, attach scab boards to stabilize it. (No.4) Cut the wedge flush or remove it.

pro tip

WHEN YOU INSTALL DRYWALL ON A CEILING, YOU CAN ORIENT PANELS EITHER PERPENDICULAR TO OR PARALLEL WITH THE CEILING JOISTS. NEITHER APPROACH MAKES TAPING THE JOINTS ANY EASIER, BUT PANELS WILL SAG LESS IF INSTALLED ACROSS THE JOISTS RATHER THAN ALIGNED WITH THEM LENGTHWISE. ON WALLS, HORIZONTAL ORIENTATION MAY NOT ONLY REDUCE THE LINEAR SEAM, BUT IT CAN MAKE TAPING EASIER BECAUSE THE JOINT FALLS APPROXIMATELY AT WAIST LEVEL.

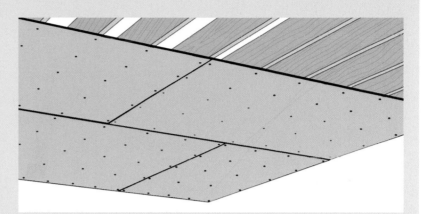

Patterns for Screws. The number of screws required depends on whether or not you use adhesive. Without adhesive, install screws every 12 in. on center; with adhesive, install every 16 in. on center.

ADDING A NICHE

POPULAR AT THE TURN OF THE CENTURY, wall niches faded away as homes became less fancy during the postwar housing boom. Although an Italian marble niche deep enough to hold a statue is going to be an expensive proposition, a simple shallow niche made from drywall or even preformed dense polyurethane is an easy addition to any partition wall, even if you haven't planned ahead for it in your framing.

It's unwise to put a niche into an exterior wall, as you'll lose insulation at that spot. The depth of your niche will be limited, then, by the depth of the partition wall (generally 3½ inches, the width of a 2x4)—although a shelf on the bottom could extend the depth enough to hold a telephone or larger vase. It's easiest to frame the niche if its width is between two studs (about 15 inches). If you wish to make a wider niche, you can cut out part of a stud, but you'll need to replace it with trimmer studs if it's a load-bearing wall (see diagram).

You can cut a niche opening in existing drywall with a reciprocating saw, or just plan it on an open stud wall. If you're cutting through drywall, you need to be careful about cutting through wires or pipes that may be behind the wall. If you're planning a wider niche, cut out that part of the stud you'll need to frame it. Install a horizontal 2x4 nailer at the top of where you want the niche to be;

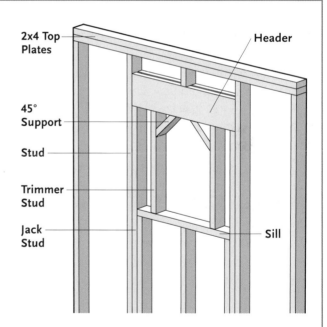

if you need to take a stud out of a load-bearing wall, install a double 2x6 or larger header instead. Install trimmer studs if you need them, and the sill, which can just be a 2x4 support or a piece of shelving with a dadoed end (or a piece of molding). If you're installing a preformed niche with an arched top, you'll need to install diagonal supports at the top to provide a nailing base for the top of the niche. Finish drywalling the rest of the wall.

ADDING FURRING TO WALLS & CEILINGS

Drywall panels are not always fastened directly to studs, joists, or old walls. Occasionally, the situation calls for furring strips to correct an out-of-level or plumb surface. Milled from softwood (spruce, pine, or fir) and sold in bundles, furring strips measure 1½ inches wide and ⅝ to 1 inch thick. Steel furring strips are also available. Furring refers to the entire process of attaching the strips and shimming them to a consistent plane.

When drywall is attached to standard-thickness furring, it stands ⅝ inch off the wall, which is ideal if the wall has an inconsistent plaster or masonry surface. Because furring is attached directly to the studs, joists, or existing surface, it may need to be shimmed at low spots in an old wall. If you come across a noticeable high spot, try to bring the bulge down if you can. Otherwise, you'll have to measure how far the bump protrudes and fur out at least that far on the rest of the surface. When adjusting for low spots, use a straightedge, level or string-and-block stand-off method to determine shim locations. (See page 48.)

Using Shims. They correct minor errors in many aspects of framing. They can be used to realign window and door frames or to even out furring strips on an uneven surface.

pro tip

FURRING IS A GREAT TIME-SAVING WAY OF FINISHING YOUR BASEMENT PERIMETER WALLS, BUT IF YOU HAVE A BASEMENT WITH MOISTURE PROBLEMS, YOU MIGHT WANT TO THINK TWICE ABOUT IT. A ROW OF NAILHOLES CAN EASILY TURN INTO A CRACK, WHICH CAN EASILY LEAD TO LEAKS—AND WATER-SOAKED DRYWALL, AMONG OTHER PROBLEMS. TO AVOID THIS, USE 2x2s OR 2x4s NOT AS FURRING BUT TO FRAME AN ENTIRELY NEW WALL. THIS CREATES ROOM FOR INSULATION, TOO.

CHOOSING THE RIGHT MASONRY FASTENER

WHEN ATTACHING WOOD TO MASONRY, you'll need special fasteners. You can choose from three basic types: hammered, powder-actuated, or shield-and-anchor.

Hammered fasteners are designed to be driven through furring and into masonry with a heavy hammer. These include spiral masonry nails and cut nails, which are heavy, flat, and tapered. Unfortunately, nails present a serious drawback: you don't have room for error when driving them. A glancing blow can loosen the nail. On the plus side, you don't have to predrill your masonry and furring strips, a requirement of shield-and-anchor systems.

Powder-actuated fasteners (PAFs) are pins that you shoot through the furring and into the masonry. This takes a special handheld tool that discharges a .22 caliber cartridge for each pin it drives. **(Use extreme caution: if a PAF is misused, the pin can act like a bullet.)** PAFs work only with concrete, not bricks or cinder blocks. The charges come in several different sizes that are color-coded to match the strength of the concrete.

Make sure you select a charge that neither overdrives the nail (through the furring strip) nor leaves the nailhead exposed. The nailhead should lie flush with or just below the furring's surface. (Experiment with different charges until you find the right one.) PAFs offer a twofold advantage: you can work very quickly, and you don't have to predrill the masonry and furring strips as you do when using a shield-and-anchor system.

Shield-and-anchor systems consist of two parts. You insert the tapered lead or plastic shields (expanding tubes) into predrilled holes in the masonry. When you drive the screws (matched to the shields) through the furring, they expand the shields, gripping the sides of the hole and resisting withdrawal.

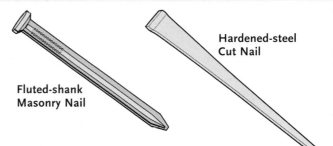

Masonry Nails. Use masonry nails and certain cut nails to drive through lumber into masonry.

Fluted-shank Masonry Nail

Hardened-steel Cut Nail

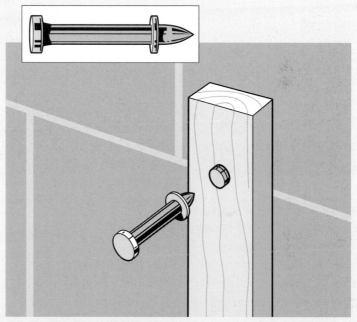

Power-Actuated Fasteners. PAFs, which are shot through wood and into masonry using a .22 caliber cartridge, are a reliable way to fasten wood to concrete. *Caution: follow manufacturer's instructions carefully.*

Specialty Bolts or Pins. These fasteners are screwed into expanding anchors. The anchors must be set in place in predrilled holes, and this requires some careful planning when spacing your furring.

Furring Over Masonry or Plaster

Difficulty Level:

TOOLS & MATERIALS

▌Furring ▌Basic hand tools ▌Chalk-line box
▌4-foot level ▌Drill & screw gun
▌Masonry bit, if anchors are used ▌Mastic adhesive
▌Caulking gun ▌Fasteners ▌String & blocks

1 Make your layout. After dampproofing, if necessary, clean the wall you intend to fur out, removing any loose masonry or plaster. Decide whether to install drywall horizontally or vertically, and then lay out your furring strips accordingly. Long strips provide a nail or screw base along the long panel edges, whereas shorter strips provide backing for end-butt joints or for the edges of vertical panels.

2 Snap chalk lines. Snap a vertical chalk line every 16 or 24 inches on center on a masonry wall. Use a level or plumb bob to make sure the chalk lines are plumb. For a plaster wall, locate the studs beneath the plaster using an electronic stud finder, and snap chalk lines on stud locations.

3 Check the wall for irregularities. Run a level or straightedge perpendicular to these chalk lines and locate any low spots or bulges. Mark them with chalk or a pencil. (See "Shimming Furring" on page 54.)

4 Prepare the furring strips. Predrill the furring strips every 16 inches for the fasteners. Hold the strips up to your chalk lines, and mark the wall where the fasteners will be located by poking through the holes with a pencil. Set the strips aside, and drill the wall for your fasteners. (You can skip these steps if you're using PAFs, masonry nails, or hardened-steel cut nails.) If your fastening system requires them, install anchor shields.

5 Attach the furring strips. Apply adhesive to the back of a strip, and using the chalk lines as a guide, place it in position. Next, use fasteners to firmly attach the two ends of the strip to the masonry. Repeat for each strip. If possible, hold off on tightening the fasteners down until you've completed the shimming.

6 Check furring for flatness. Using a straightedge, level, or string-and-block standoff method, check to see that your furring strips form a flat surface.

1 Furring is an ideal nailing base to install over masonry surfaces. It can be easily shimmed to present a plumb plane on which to attach drywall panels.

4 Hold the predrilled furring strip in position, make sure it's plumb, and use the holes to mark where to drill for bolt anchors.

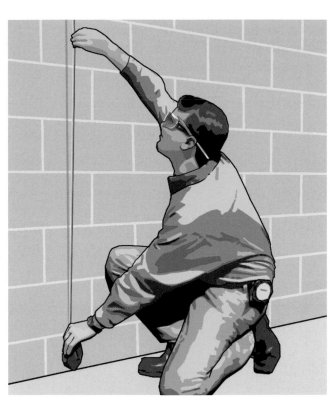

2 To properly position furring on a masonry wall, snap chalk lines, left, at the proper on-center spacing (based on your 16- or 24-in.-on-center layout marks) to guide furring placement. (When furring over an old plaster wall, match the on-center spacing of the studs beneath.)

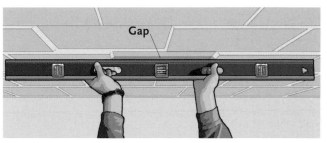

Gap

3 To determine whether shimming is required behind furring strips, place a straightedge on the wall to see whether there is a gap behind it. If so, the wall is recessed at this point, and shimming may be required.

5 After inserting shields or anchors (if used), apply construction adhesive to the backs of the furring strips, and then attach the ends of each strip.

6 Finish attaching the furring strips to the wall (shimming where needed), using screws, nails, or PAFs. (See "Choosing the Right Masonry Fastener," on page 51.)

Furring Stud Walls

Attaching furring strips directly to framing ensures that the nailing surface for drywall is as level (for ceilings) or plumb (for walls) as possible. A remodeling job will usually expose old and sometimes irregular framing. Newly framed structures or rooms may not require furring (depending on the quality of the lumber and the skill of the framing crew). In either situation, you may want to install furring strips if you suspect that studs or joists are out of true, which could ruin the job.

When attaching furring strips to existing framing, install them perpendicular to the framing members. In walls, this means the furring will be horizontal, which will require horizontal placement of drywall panels. In ceilings, the strips will run across (rather than along) the joists. This will have little bearing on the orientation of the panels, or on which way the joints run.

Furring Over Stud and Joist Framing

Difficulty Level:

TOOLS & MATERIALS
- Chalk-line box ▪ 4-foot level ▪ Basic hand tools
- Furring and shims ▪ Plumb bob
- Screw gun or drill ▪ String and blocks
- 2½-inch common nails or dry wall screws

Between the ends of the furring strips (for instance, along the top and bottom of the wall), you'll need to install filler furring to provide a nail base for panel edges along the ends of the wall. This will ensure that all drywall edges and ends will be solidly backed.

SHIMMING FURRING

WHETHER YOU'RE DRYWALLING over masonry, framing, or old plaster, it's imperative that you create a surface that is both flat and plumb (for walls) or level (for ceilings). By inserting shims (cedar shingles) behind furring strips before fastening them down, you can compensate for any low spots in a wall. This simple process involves three steps: detecting low spots, shimming them one by one, and then screwing or nailing the strips permanently in place.

Once you've snapped chalk lines to lay out your furring, survey the wall for obvious low spots by holding a straightedge (a 4-foot level) against the wall. Orient it in the same direction that your furring strips will run. Mark any low spots along the length of your chalk lines.

Install the furring strips, but fasten them only at the ends. Using the string-and-block standoff method, determine which strips protrude or recede. At the receding (low) spots, insert shims behind the strips. For large gaps, use opposing shims. (See the drawing at right.)

Finally, drive nails or screws through the furring strips and shims into the framing.

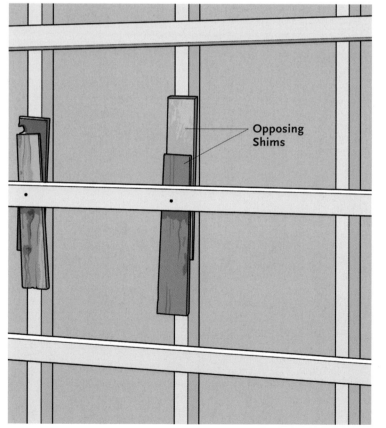

Opposing Shims

Checking the Furring. Use a level or string and blocks to check your furring for low spots, and shim those areas up to the correct plane of the rest of the wall.

1 **Lay out your lines on the studs.** Determine the spacing for your furring, either 16 or 24 inches on center. (If you have a choice, go with 16 inches, which will make the drywall more rigid.) On walls, snap chalk lines at the proper intervals, using a level and measuring tape to position them accurately. On ceilings, lay out the spacing with a measuring tape, and then snap chalk lines across the undersides of the joists.

2 **Check the wall for straightness.** For walls, use a level (or any long straightedge) to check for irregularities in the framing members. Mark the recesses or bulges on the edge of the studs. Use the same procedure for checking the ceiling framing.

3 **Install the horizontal furring strips.** Attach the horizontal furring strips, but screw or nail just the ends so that the strips can be easily shimmed. Using the string-and-block standoff method and noting your pencil marks from the previous step, shim the furring or shave the framing (high spots) as necessary to achieve a flat plane.

4 **Install the vertical strips and shims.** Install shorter strips where the ends of the drywall will fall. Leave a ¼-inch gap at each end where the vertical strips meet the horizontal ones. (Use 14-inch short strips between 16-inch on-center horizontal furring, or 22-inch short strips between 24-inch on-center furring.) Shim the furring as necessary, and then fasten the strips into place.

1 Mark the position of furring strips on the studs by snapping chalk lines based on your layout marks.

2 Use a straightedge to check the wall for irregularities. Any recesses may have to be shimmed.

3 Install the horizontal furring strips, but screw down just the ends so they can be easily shimmed.

4 Attach the filler furring strips between the main courses of furring, and then fasten.

Installing Metal Furring on a Ceiling

Difficulty Level:

TOOLS & MATERIALS
▍ String, blocks, and shims
▍ Chalk-line box
▍ Resilient metal channels
▍ Aviation snips ▍ Screw gun
▍ Sheet-metal screws ▍ 4-ft. level

1 Lay out for the ceiling channels, in this case 16 in. on center, and then snap chalk lines.

You have several options when it comes to installing a ceiling in the basement. You can hang a suspended ceiling, which uses a grid to hold acoustical tiles. This option might be better if you must have access to utilities like electrical or plumbing and you can afford to lose a few inches of headroom. According to most building codes, each room in a finished basement must have a minimum of 90 inches of headroom (84 inches in kitchens, hallways, and bathrooms) over at least half of its area.

If headroom is tight, you should install drywall and paint it or glue acoustical tile to it. Don't attach drywall directly to the underside of the ceiling joists, however; use resilient steel furring channels attached perpendicular to the joists and shimmed where needed.

2 You may need to cut the furring strips to fit. Use aviation or metal snips to cut the flanges of the metal strip; then bend it back and cut across the webbing.

1 Check and mark the joists. In some basements the ceiling joists may be inconsistent—this can cause an unevenness in the finished surface. Before you install the ceiling channel tracks, use the string-and-block method to check for level, and note any high spots, which you'll have to shave, or low spots, which you'll have to shim. Then snap chalk lines across the joists at 16 or 24 inches on-center to act as guidelines for installing the metal furring.

2 Cut the furring. If you need to cut the furring to fit the width of the ceiling, use aviation snips to cut the two flanges; then bend back the track and cut the web.

3 Install the furring. Set a ceiling channel track in place along your chalk lines, and attach it by driving 1½-inch drywall nails or screws into the flanges on each side at each joist. As you install the channel, use a level to double-check for consistency from row to row. Shim where necessary. When furring is level, use screws to apply drywall as you would to any ceiling.

3 Screw the ceiling channels into place along the guidelines. Use a 4-ft. level to ensure that the channels are in a level plane.

SOUNDPROOFING

GYPSUM WALLBOARD alone has sound-deadening properties, but in some situations you may want to add extra protection from noise—for example, in the wall between a shop and living areas or between a bedroom and kitchen. Sound passes between rooms through any small opening, and walls, floors, and ceilings transmit vibrations. Your first step is to seal up any openings. Once you've taken care of those, you can use a number of different techniques to deaden vibrations.

■ If your shop or garage is unfinished, fill the bays between studs with batts of fiberglass insulation, and cover the unfinished side with ½-inch or thicker wallboard. This alone will eliminate a great deal of noise on the other side of the wall.

■ Even better, install a second layer on the shop side—preferably on top of steel hat channel. These metal tracks raise a panel off the surface below, keeping the topmost panel from transmitting the sound efficiently to the surface beneath it. Install the channels horizontally 6 inches below the ceiling and 2 inches above the floor, no more than 2 feet apart.

■ Instead of installing a second layer of drywall, try adding acoustical tiles to the noisy side of the partition. Simply spread adhesive on the back of the panels and screw them down, using fasteners long enough to penetrate into the framing beneath. This material will provide even more noise reduction than drywall.

■ If you're building a new structure and can plan ahead for it, staggered-stud framing offers excellent sound-deadening qualities. For this technique, use a 2x6 plate, and align adjacent 2x4 studs with opposite edges of the plate, 12 inches on center. Weave fiberglass insulation into the gap between the studs. The two faces of the wall have no direct contact with each other, except at the top and bottom plates, which reduces noise transmission even more.

■ A layer of acoustical tile or specially made sound-deadening board, when sandwiched between layers of ½-inch-thick drywall, is just as effective at deadening sound transmission as a staggered-stud wall; it will make even the loudest machinery (or people) barely audible on the other side.

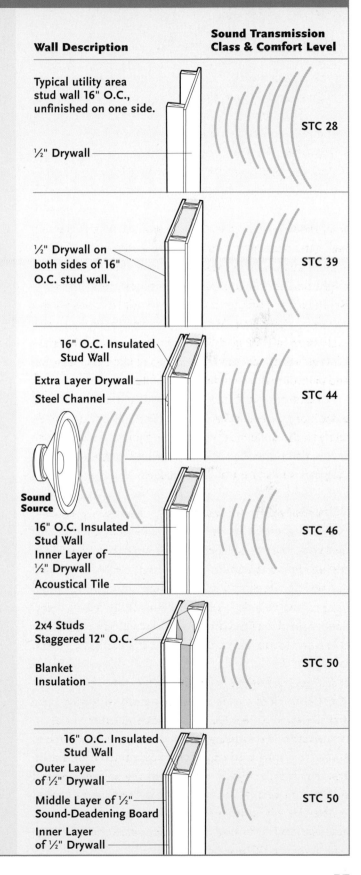

Wall Description	Sound Transmission Class & Comfort Level
Typical utility area stud wall 16" O.C., unfinished on one side. ½" Drywall	STC 28
½" Drywall on both sides of 16" O.C. stud wall.	STC 39
16" O.C. Insulated Stud Wall Extra Layer Drywall Steel Channel Sound Source	STC 44
16" O.C. Insulated Stud Wall Inner Layer of ½" Drywall Acoustical Tile	STC 46
2x4 Studs Staggered 12" O.C. Blanket Insulation	STC 50
16" O.C. Insulated Stud Wall Outer Layer of ½" Drywall Middle Layer of ½" Sound-Deadening Board Inner Layer of ½" Drywall	STC 50

STEEL FRAMING SYSTEMS

Steel-Framed Walls

Steel has long been the material of choice for commercial buildings, but not for houses. However, while lumber prices increase and lumber quality decreases, both the cost and strength of steel has stayed steady.

Steel doesn't warp, shrink, or split like wood, and it isn't food for insects. It won't rot from water leaks—though it may corrode over long exposure. Steel doesn't make a house fireproof, but it won't contribute fuel to a fire, and it keeps the structure intact long after a burning wood frame would collapse. That's one reason why metal framing is standard in commercial construction. Unlike lumber, which can be—and these days increasingly is—riddled with defects, steel studs are never warped, checked, or green.

Even well-built modern homes with wood frames are likely to undergo some shifting and settling that can pop drywall nails and trim joints—or worse. These problems are greatly reduced with steel. It doesn't hold water, so metal studs won't shrink and twist the way wood often does, particularly in the first year after construction when wet wood dries out during the heating season. Also, steel framing members are lighter than solid wood, and put less load on the foundation, which can reduce cracking and faults in masonry as well.

Residential steel construction initially caught on along the West Coast, where the extra strength was valuable against earthquakes, and then in the Southeast to resist damage from hurricanes. It continues, gradually, to gain favor with contractors and homebuyers. Fewer than 15,000 houses were built with steel framing in 1993, but 11 years later it was closer to 200,000.

Typical steel construction involves 20-gauge metal studs about the shape of 2×4s, but with one open side (like a letter C in cross section). These studs are attached (generally with sheet-metal screws) to U-shaped tracks attached to the floor and ceiling. In situations with concrete floors, the bottom track is easily secured with powder-actuated fasteners (PAFs). Steel studs are generally spaced 16 to 24 inches on center, the same as wood framing. These light-gauge studs are only used for non-load-bearing interior walls; they're not strong enough to support loads (without being sistered together). But a do-

Steel Framing Advantages. The material has its advantages, among them the ability to easily execute custom effects such as this multilevel ceiling.

it-yourselfer without experience in steel construction can easily use steel systems to construct partition walls—and at a lower cost than lumber. Large drywall-supply houses will usually carry steel-framing supplies.

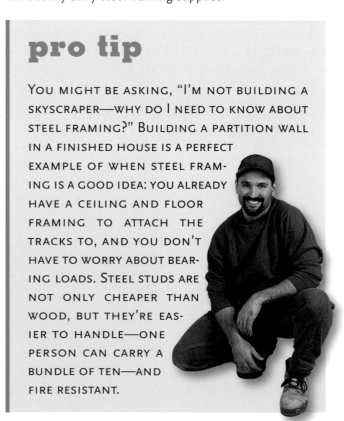

pro tip

You might be asking, "I'm not building a skyscraper—why do I need to know about steel framing?" Building a partition wall in a finished house is a perfect example of when steel framing is a good idea: you already have a ceiling and floor framing to attach the tracks to, and you don't have to worry about bearing loads. Steel studs are not only cheaper than wood, but they're easier to handle—one person can carry a bundle of ten—and fire resistant.

PREPARING STEEL FRAMING FOR DRYWALL

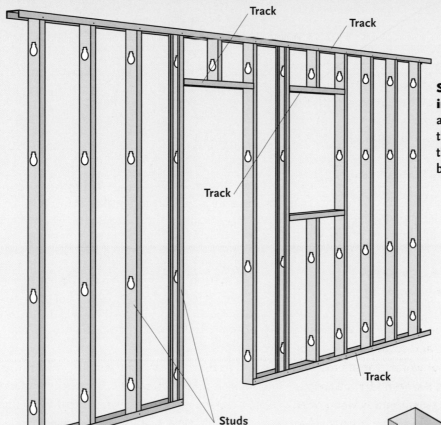

Track

Track

Track

Track

Standard Steel Framing. Headers, plates, and sills are cut from the track, which takes the place of the top and bottom plates.

Studs

Stud Configuration. Studs have one open side with ¼-in. lips; the web side of studs have holes precut to allow for wires.

Steel Stud

Web Side

Open Side

Track

Self-Tapping Sheet-Metal Screw

THERE IS ONLY MINIMAL PREPARATION before attaching drywall to steel-framed walls. You should check the framing for straightness as you would with wood (although it's most likely going to be straight). You'll also have to check the orientation of the studs themselves. The open side of the C-shaped channels should all be facing in the same direction.

You'll install the panels of a wall starting in the corner that the open end of the stud faces. If you install the panels in the opposite direction, to the solid side first and then the open side, the screw might bend the open end outward, causing the panels to abut unevenly. Use bugle-head screws with self-tapping points to install the drywall—ordinary drywall screws are capable of drilling through 20-gauge steel, but in the process they will dig out a hole in the drywall larger than the head of the screw, creating finishing problems and unstable drywall.

The panels should ideally all be cut so that the edges break exactly halfway across the stud. If you need to add blocking, clip away the ¼-inch lip that forms the mouth of the "C," and screw a piece of plywood on the inside of the studs. For more detail on installing drywall on steel studs, see "Installing Drywall on a Steel-Framed Wall," pages 94–95.

SUSPENDED CEILINGS

If you want to install a perfectly flat ceiling over old drywall with a hilly topography—or even over brand-new framing that seems out of whack—using a steel-frame suspended ceiling system might turn out to be easier than endlessly fussing with furring and shims. Modern suspension systems are substantially easier to install than old systems.

Installing a Suspended Ceiling System

Difficulty Level: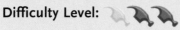

TOOLS & MATERIALS
▎ Basic hand tools ▎ Measuring tape ▎ Water level
▎ 4-foot level ▎ Resilient metal channels
▎ Hanger ties ▎ Screw gun ▎ Aviation snips
▎ Screws (sheet-metal and drywall Type S)

1 Install the track. Using a water level, mark the desired elevation where you want the drywall to go. (Keep in mind that the drywall will be ½ to ⅝ inch below the suspension system, and that most building codes require at least 90 inches of headroom in normal living spaces.) Now mark the line where you will install the track, which will support the ceiling framing. Install the track—either channel molding (which is C-shaped) or wall angle (which is L-shaped)—into the studs at the top of the wall using sheet-metal screws.

2 Install the main tees. Main tees generally come in 10- or 12-foot lengths. If one of your room's dimensions happens to be 10 or 12 feet, make this the dimension across which you will place the main tees. Otherwise, you will have to cut the main tees to fit a shorter dimension or splice two of them together (using hanger wire or specially-made splicing clips available where you purchase the tees) to fit a longer dimension. Place the main tees on the track every 2 feet. Check the tees for level, and then attach the hanger wires from the main tees to the existing ceiling joists, to provide additional support for the ceiling.

3 Install the cross tees. Install the cross tees perpendicular to the main tees every 16 or 24 inches on center. (Cross tees are manufactured in 2-foot lengths to fit in between the main tees.) This will provide a level surface and sufficient support for drywalling. (See pages 82–85.)

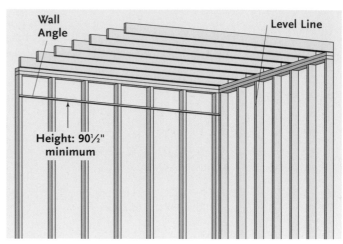

1 After you've marked the elevation with a level, you're ready to install the track around the perimeter of the room. Screw it into the studs using metal screws.

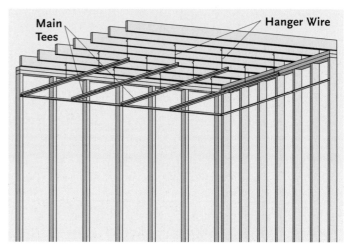

2 Main tees will be installed 24 in. on center. Cut or splice them to the proper length, and snap them into the track. Attach hanger wires for additional support.

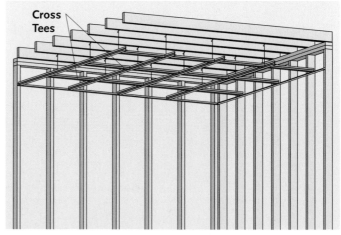

3 Cross tees are installed under the main tees every 16 or 24 in. on center. They come in 24-in. lengths to fit between the main tees.

SUSPENDED DRYWALL FASCIA & SCULPTURED CEILINGS

ADVANCES IN BOTH suspension systems and flexible drywall have permitted designers to be much more adventurous in their use of curves—not just in walls, but in multilevel ceilings and serpentine soffit boxes. It's something that is most effective when used minimally, but a room can be given a great deal of flair at minimal expense—without having a frame of fancy curves in wood—with the addition of an undulating corner or recessed ceiling panel. Think of them as partial dropped ceilings. Special curved main tees and trim are available, so any shape can be dropped down from the main joists: circles, serpentine boxes, any kind of shape you can imagine.

Special Effects. Suspended ceiling systems make it easy to add a sculptural effect to your ceiling with elegant soffits.

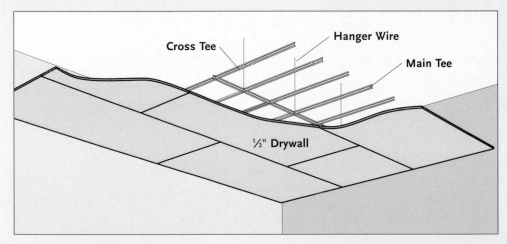

Cross Tee

Hanger Wire

Main Tee

½" Drywall

Simple Ceilings. Metal suspended ceiling systems require no special equipment to install. Lightweight steel is screwed into a track and tied to existing joists with hanger wire. Suspension systems are usually compatible with acoustical tiles, lighting panels, and drywall.

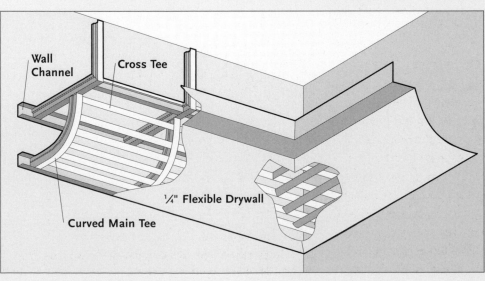

Wall Channel

Cross Tee

¼" Flexible Drywall

Curved Main Tee

Curved Soffits. Create curved soffits with metal suspension systems. Just use the curved main tees (visible at left) spaced 48 in. on center, and space the regular cross tees tighter (9 in. on center). Curved cross tees are also available for making S-shape boxes. Just follow the recommendation for installing drywall on curved walls (pages 96–97).

Continued on next page.

Continued from previous page.

SUSPENDED DRYWALL FASCIA & SCULPTURED CEILINGS

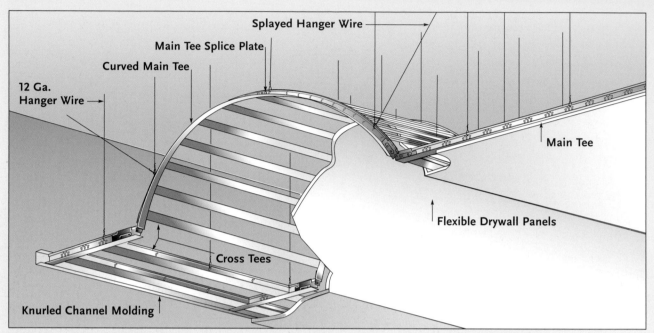

Soaring Ceilings. Vaults provide a distinctive design touch and are a good way to customize any drywall application. Place hanger wires a maximum of 48 in. along the main tee. For stability, drywall joints should be a minimum of 12 in. from main tee splices.

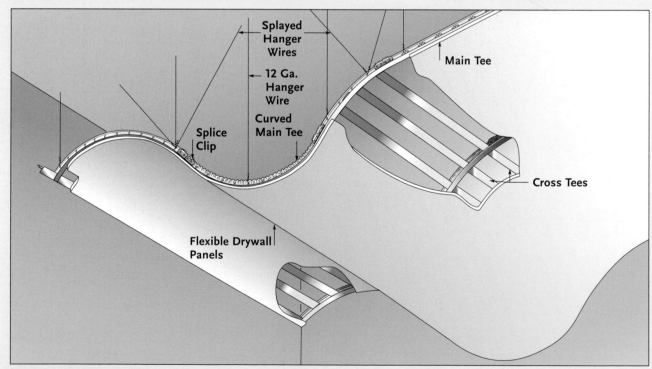

Vaults and Valleys. Use a metal suspension system to create vaults and valleys, such as the one shown here. Splayed hanger wires add stability to the curved sections of drywall. For curved sections, use flexible drywall panels recommended by the manufacturer.

There's no deep secret to measuring and marking drywall, but a few tricks of the trade and specialty tools will streamline your efforts and improve your accuracy. Once you've got the hang of marking holes and angles, you can test the various tools and techniques to aid you in making precise (and, where possible, dustless) cuts in drywall panels.

STRAIGHT CUTS

Marking straight cut lines on drywall requires a keen eye and the right tools. A straight cut line usually refers to one that is square to an edge or end of the panel. Because the manufacturer's edge serves as a dependable reference, most methods for squaring lines on drywall rely on this edge as a guide. The following procedure calls for a T-square, but you can also use a smaller tool, such as a combination or framing square. Before you begin to make any cuts, ensure that the tool you are using is actually straight by sighting down its length.

Straight Cut Lines. For short, straight cuts in a piece of drywall, a sharp drywall or utility saw and a steady cutting motion are all that is needed.

pro tip

ON A T-SQUARE, BOTH THE BLADE AND THE FENCE HAVE RULE MARKS STENCILED ON THEM THAT START WITH ZERO AT THE INSIDE CORNER OF THE SQUARE. MOST PEOPLE BEGIN A JOB BY USING THE T-SQUARE AS A GUIDE FOR DRAWING A CUT LINE FIRST. BUT AS YOU GET ACCUSTOMED TO WORKING WITH A T-SQUARE, YOU CAN SIMPLY CUT ALONG THE BLADE EDGE WITH YOUR UTILITY KNIFE, STOPPING WHEN YOU GET TO THE NEEDED MEASUREMENT (ANYWHERE FROM AN INCH TO 4 FEET), AND SKIP THE STEP OF PENCIL-MARKING THE CUT LINE.

Cutting Drywall

Marking Cut Lines Using a T-Square

Difficulty Level:

TOOLS & MATERIALS
▌ Drywall panels
▌ Measuring tape or folding rule
▌ Pencil
▌ 4-foot T-square
▌ Utility knife

Drywall panels are easy to cut. You will find that a sharp utility knife will make most of the cuts necessary for just about any project. Keep a supply of spare blades on hand because drywall will dull a blade quickly. Once you have determined where the panel will be cut, score the cut line with the utility knife. That will be enough to allow you to snap the panel apart with just a thin layer of paper on the back side of the panel holding it together. Cut the paper to separate the sections of the panel.

1 Measure your cut lines. Stand the drywall panel upright. Use a measuring tape to determine the size of the piece you need, and then locate these dimensions on the drywall panel.

2 Mark the lines on the panel. Place the 4-foot T-square against the panel so that the long blade is parallel with the cut line you intend to make. Slide the T-square along the edge or end of the panel until the edge of its blade lines up with the mark you made. Run your pencil along the blade, marking your cut line. Repeat this step for the perpendicular cut line, if one is needed. Before making any cut, make sure your utility knife has a sharp blade, and wear eye protection. Using a straightedge as your guide, score the face (good) side of the drywall to a depth of ⅛ inch.

3 Snap the cut back. Working from the cut side (or the side opposite the cut), use a quick motion to snap the panel along the cut line, and fold it back slightly. You can also bump the back of the sheet at the cut line with your knee as you hold the sheet. Don't try to tear the cut panel; just let the panel break along your cut line. The panel should now be held together just by the paper backing. Using the utility knife, cut through the paper on the back, and separate the pieces.

1 Use the measurements you took from the wall, and transfer them onto the panel you intend to install. One mark at the top of the panel is usually sufficient.

2 Using the T-square, first draw your cut line on the face of the panel. Then, using your foot to seat the bottom of the square, make the cut using a utility knife.

3 Using one motion, snap the panel back along the cut line. Cut through the paper on the back of the panel, and separate the pieces (inset).

Marking Cut Lines Using a Chalk Line

Difficulty Level:

TOOLS & MATERIALS
▌Drywall panels ▌Measuring tape or folding rule
▌Pencil ▌Chalk-line box ▌Utility knife

Snapping a chalk line marks a long, straight line quickly and accurately. It works especially well on diagonal lines. The trick is to locate and mark dimensions on the adjacent edge and end of a panel, and then snap a chalk line between them.

1 **Measure your cut lines.** Using a measuring tape, locate the dimensions of the drywall piece you require onto opposite edges or ends of the drywall panel.

2 **Snap chalk lines on the panel.** Using these reference marks, snap chalk lines across the full length or width (or diagonal) of the panel.

3 **Cut the lines.** Using a utility knife, score and snap cut lines as described on the previous page.

1 Locate the dimensions of the piece you need onto a panel or piece of a panel.

2 If necessary, seat the string in a small notch made on the first mark. Run the chalk line between the two marks, and snap it, leaving a straight chalk mark.

3 Using your utility knife, cut the line you have made. Snap the panel back along the cut line, and then cut from the back.

Cutting Drywall

For most walls, you have to make cutouts for utility boxes (outlets and fixtures), switches, pipes, and services such as ductwork. You should always double-check before installing a panel. If you miss a cutout, you'll have to take down the drywall. If just the subflooring has been installed, you may want to mark the location of each light switch and power outlet on the plywood using a permanent marker. You could do the same using masking tape on finished flooring or carpeting.

To use the coordinate method for marking and cutting holes, treat the drywall panel as if it were a piece of graph paper. To locate a point or outline a box, draw intersecting lines from an adjacent edge and end of the panel.

1 Locate the required hole on the panel. On the wall where you'll attach the drywall panel, measure to the near sides of the switch or receptacle box you must accommodate. To get accurate dimensions, start your measurements at the corner and ceiling (or floor) against which the panel will finally sit. Then lay out these dimensions on the panel: for example, 25 inches in from the right and 32 inches down from the top. For a round hole, you'll need to note only the centerpoint of the circle. For a rectangular cutout, measure to the far sides of the box, and then transfer all four sides to the piece of drywall.

2 Draw the outline of the hole on the panel. Using the 4-foot T-square or a measuring tape, connect the coordinate points of the box on the panel face. If you have an identical utility box nearby, measure to the far corner point of the existing box, line up the spare one with the point, and trace a pencil outline around the box.

3 Cut out the hole. Drill a starter hole through one corner of the box or near the circle's perimeter, and then cut along the line with a utility knife or saw. Hold the panel in place to verify that the hole lines up with the box. Trim the hole to enlarge it if necessary.

1 By finding the X and Y coordinates for a utility box, you can transfer those measurements to the drywall and precisely cut out a rectangle to fit the box.

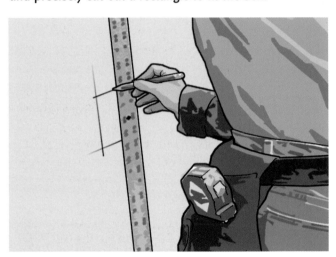

2 Use a T-square to transfer your coordinate measurements to the panel, and draw a box to be cut away. (Or trace the outline of a spare box.)

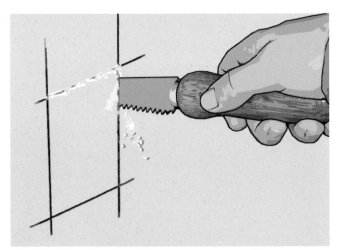

3 Cut out the piece. Be sure the cutout section is precise; inaccurately cut corners can result in face damage when the drywall is pushed into place.

Using the Hammer-and-Block Method

Difficulty Level:

TOOLS & MATERIALS

▌ Hammer ▌ 8-inch 2x4 block ▌ Utility saw

Because drywall is relatively soft, it shows indentations where objects have hit or pressed against it. Here's a method for marking utility boxes that takes advantage of this characteristic.

1 **Set the panel in place.** Before making any utility-box cutouts, place the drywall panel in position against the studs or wall, just as if you were installing it.

2 **Tap the panel over the utility boxes.** Place a piece of scrap wood against the panel wherever a box is located, and tap the wood lightly with a hammer. The edges of the box should make a slight indentation in the panel's back face.

3 **Cut out the hole.** Remove the drywall panel, jab a utility saw through one of the corners of the indentation, and then cut out the opening. Reinstall the panel, and fasten it in place.

1 An alternative method of marking for a utility box is to position the drywall where it will be installed, and then place a block over the box's location.

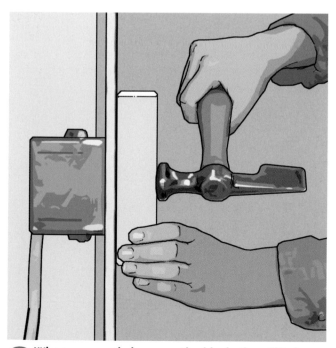

2 When you gently hammer the block, the utility box will leave an imprint on the back of the drywall panel, indicating the shape to be cut out.

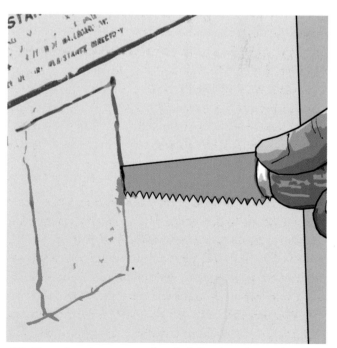

3 Turn the sheet around and, following the outline, carefully cut out the hole using a utility saw. Be careful not to damage the face.

CURVED CUTS

Arched doorways and areas around fancy window wells often require curved cuts. The simplest way to make these cuts is to install the full panel over them and trim the excess by following a utility saw along the top of the curve. Sometimes this isn't possible, such as when a window has already been installed and there's no room to move a saw. To mark these curves with accuracy, you can use a string or make yourself a cardboard template.

If an archway has a consistent curve, it's part of a perfect circle (an arc). If you can determine that circle's radius (the distance from the centerpoint to the circumference), you can draw any part of it using a pencil and string. You may want to practice it first on cardboard—cut along the arc with a utility knife, and compare the resulting template with the area you intend to drywall. (If it fits, simply use it to mark the actual panel.)

If your archway has a flattened or asymmetrical curve, move on to "Marking a Curve Using a Template," page 48.

Curves and Irregular Lines. Cutting curves into panels before they're installed can be tricky; it's easier to trim them in place if possible.

Marking a Semicircle with String

Difficulty Level: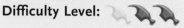

TOOLS & MATERIALS
▌ Measuring tape
▌ Drywall panel
▌ Pencil
▌ Nonstretchable string
▌ Utility knife
▌ Masking tape
▌ Utility saw

Measuring and cutting a large circular line on a drywall panel doesn't have to be difficult or require specialized equipment. A simple measuring tool made from string and a pencil—plus a bit of practice— is often all you need.

1 **Determine the radius of the arch.** For a half-circle, just measure the width of the door and divide by 2; for less than a half-circle, use the method described on page 98. Tie a pencil to a length of nonstretchable string; then mark the radius along the string using a piece of masking tape.

2 **Transfer the arch to the drywall.** Establish the center of the circle on the panel, and hold the string at the tape mark on that point with your thumb. With the string fully extended, swing the pencil across the panel, drawing a curved line that matches your archway. Score the line repeatedly with a utility knife, or use a utility saw to cut out the piece.

1 To determine the radius of an arc forming a half-circle, first measure the diameter, and then divide by 2. In our example, the diameter is 3 ft. The 18-in. radius can then be transferred to the string and pencil.

2 Transfer the arc onto a piece of drywall by tacking (or holding with your thumb) the string at one edge of the drywall and swinging the pencil at the limit of the string to the right and left, drawing a curved line.

Cutting Drywall

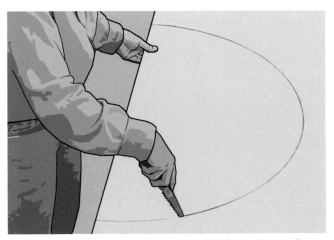

Marking a Curve Using a Template

Difficulty Level:

TOOLS & MATERIALS
▌Cardboard ▌Pencil ▌Drywall panel
▌Utility knife ▌Utility saw

You'll often encounter archways that are not circles. These curves might be slightly flattened (or flat) at the top, or parts of ellipses or parabolas rather than circles. In these cases, use a cardboard template to transfer the curve onto the drywall.

1 **Make a cardboard template.** Hold a piece of cardboard against the curve, and trace its shape. You can trace a window frame only if the window has not yet been installed. If the window is already in place, cut a rough template, and trim it as needed until it fits the archway exactly.

2 **Use the template to mark the drywall.** Place the cardboard template on the panel exactly where the curve will occur, and then trace the shape. Use a T-square or chalk-line box to mark any other required cuts.

3 **Cut out the archway.** Score the cut line repeatedly using a utility knife, or use a utility saw to make the cutout; then install the panel.

1 To create a template, hold a piece of cardboard up to the archway, trace the archway's shape, and cut the cardboard.

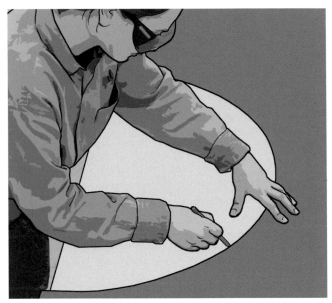

2 Position the template on a piece of drywall where the archway will occur in the final drywall panel installation, and trace the template's shape.

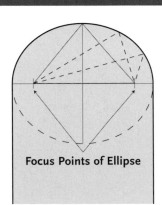

WHEN TO USE A TEMPLATE

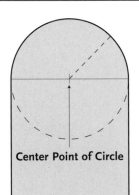

Center Point of Circle   Focus Points of Ellipse

Cutting Ellipses. Some curves are not arcs of perfect circles but of ellipses (which have two focal points). The string method is more complicated when used for cutting these curves. It is best to create a template to copy the shape of the arc.

3 After tracing the archway's shape from the cardboard onto the drywall, use a utility knife or saw to cut out the shape.

Marking a Round Hole

Difficulty Level:

TOOLS & MATERIALS
▌Drywall panel ▌Measuring tape or 4-foot T-square
▌Pencil ▌Compass ▌Utility saw

Many light fixtures are mounted on (or hang from) square or octagonal utility boxes. For these shapes, use the coordinate method described earlier to draw the cutout. Other fixtures require round holes, as do pipes and some types of ductwork.

1 **Measure for the round hole.** Use a measuring tape and the coordinate method to determine where the centerpoint of the round hole will fall on the panel you are going to install. (See "Using the Coordinate Method for Marking and Cutting Openings," page 44.) Next, determine the radius of the hole by measuring across the entire width of the fixture or the pipe or duct that you're cutting out for and dividing this measurement by 2.

2 **Draw the hole on the drywall.** Set the point of a compass on the centerpoint you've marked and the arm at the radius measurement. Draw the circle onto the drywall.

3 **Cut out the hole.** Use a utility knife, circle cutter, or utility saw to cut the hole.

1 To cut out a circle in a piece of drywall, first find the coordinates for the center of the circle, and determine the circle's radius. Transfer the centerpoint of the circle to the drywall.

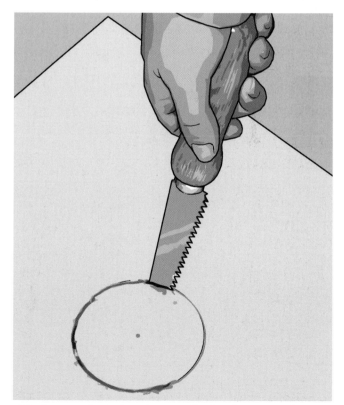

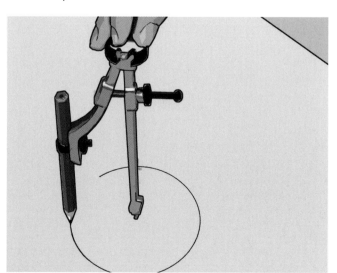

2 Use a compass to mark the circle on the panel. For larger circles, use the string method, page 47, or a circle cutter, page 50.

3 Cut out the hole using a utility knife or saw. If the hole isn't too small or too large for a circle cutter, you can cut it out more accurately using that tool.

SPECIAL TECHNIQUES FOR MARKING & CUTTING

Scribing Drywall to an Irregular Wall

Occasionally, drywall abuts or adjoins an irregular wall: a fieldstone hearth, a brick wall, or an out-of-true plaster wall. These situations call for scribing, using a compass or special scriber, which makes it easy to transfer an irregular profile onto a panel.

To do this, position a drywall panel next to the irregular wall or structure exactly as it will sit but an inch or two back from its installed location. Slide the pointed end of the scriber down the irregular profile, keeping it firmly in contact with the masonry or plaster so that the scriber's pencil faithfully reproduces the profile on the face of the panel. Cut along this line using a utility knife or saw.

You can make nearly all cuts in drywall using a sharp utility knife. However, certain specialty tools offer more accuracy and convenience than the knife, particularly for cutting circular holes. There's also a short-cut method for cutting out holes for pipe.

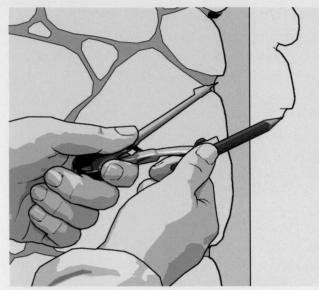

Scribing Drywall. To scribe drywall to an irregular wall, first position the drywall panel square to the wall, and stabilize it so that it doesn't move when you draw on it. Then run a scribe down the face of the irregular wall so that a profile of the wall is drawn on the drywall's face with the scribe's pencil.

Using a Circle Cutter and a Hole Saw

If you're installing a ceiling panel over recessed lighting, which usually calls for several identical, perfectly round holes, you'll want a streamlined technique for cutting them. Instead of pencil and string, use a circle cutter for larger holes—and chuck a hole saw into a drill for small ones.

A circle cutter resembles a beam compass, except that it has a sharp cutting edge instead of a pencil at the end of its adjustable beam. You set the circle cutter's pin at the layout mark on the panel; adjust the beam to the desired radius; and then rotate to cut a perfect circle. (For a quicker job, you can also buy a circle cutter that chucks into a portable drill.)

For a series of small holes (and, unfortunately, big clouds of dust), you can load your drill with a special bit called a hole saw. These cylindrical bits have serrated teeth on one end and a shaft that fits your drill chuck on the other. Hole saws cannot be adjusted for size, so you buy them in sets that cover a range of diameters.

Circle Cutters. A circle cutter is an ideal tool for cutting perfect circles in a drywall panel. A pin at the center anchors the tool, and the compass arm has a round blade that scores a perfect circle into drywall. The tool can be adjusted to cut circles of different diameters.

Making a Cutout with a Router

Just as routers can be used to cut holes in wood, so they can also be used (with a large Forstner or spur bit) to make cutouts in drywall. Use the coordinate or hammer-and-block method to mark the hole location, and then apply the router to the task. It kicks up more dust than manual cutting, but it's fast and accurate.

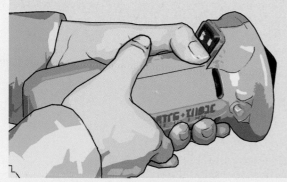

Using a Router. A router can make cutouts for utility boxes when fitted with a bit designed for drywall. This is best done with the drywall in place.

Using a Hole Saw. A hole saw can be attached to any electric drill to cut perfect small holes.

RECYCLING DRYWALL

ONCE YOU'VE FINISHED your drywalling job, you may wonder whether anything beneficial might be done with the considerable heap of scrap gypsum board that you've generated. In fact, you may not have the option of ignoring the problem. Some municipalities have started banning gypsum drywall from their landfills because it releases hydrogen sulfide gas as it breaks down.

There are companies that will collect scrap drywall for recycling, but most require that it be free of nails, screws, lead paint, and asbestos. Happily, many drywall manufacturers are now producing wallboard that contains at least some post-consumer recycled gypsum, and the paper backing is often made with recycled paper.

Some drywall is now being buried in cornfields rather than landfills. Farmers have long added pure gypsum (calcium sulfate) to the soil to improve fertility and keep the pH stable. Agricultural researchers have substituted pulverized wallboard—paper and all—and found that it contributes the same benefits as pure gypsum or limestone without the heavy metals or other unwanted by-products. Farms in Colorado and California are already using recycled gypsum board for certain food crops.

pro tip

YOU CAN CREATE LARGE CIRCLES USING NON-STRETCHABLE STRING. LOCATE THE CENTER OF THE CIRCLE, AND THEN TIE A PENCIL ON THE END OF A STRING THAT IS A LITTLE LONGER THAN THE CIRCLE'S RADIUS. PIN THE OTHER END OF THE STRING (MEASURED FOR THE RADIUS) AT THE CENTER OF THE CIRCLE, AND KEEP THE STRING TAUT AS YOU TRACE THE CIRCLE.

Cutting a Pipe Hole with Pipe

Difficulty Level:

TOOLS & MATERIALS
▪ Measuring tape or folding rule
▪ 4-foot T-square
▪ Pencil
▪ Drill with ⅛-inch masonry bit
▪ Hammer
▪ 12-inch section of pipe

When installing cement-based board in a bathroom, you'll have to cut holes through which the pipes can protrude. When cutting out for these pipes, you can use a leftover piece of the pipe itself as a tool.

1 Mark the hole on the drywall. Use the coordinate method to locate and mark the center of where the pipe hole will go. (See "Using the Coordinate Method for Marking and Cutting Openings," page 44.) Draw a circle of the same diameter as your pipe centered on this mark. Use the discarded piece of the pipe as your template. (You can also use a compass.)

2 Perforate the hole. Using an 8d nail or a power drill with a ⅛- to ¼-inch masonry bit, perforate the circumference of this circle, driving the nail or drilling through the panel. Make at least 16 or 20 holes around the circumference of the circle—not so many that the holes are touching, but enough the make the circle easy to break.

3 Punch out the hole using the pipe. Place the panel on firm backing; then drive a piece of pipe (optimally with sharp edges) through the drywall panel using a hammer.

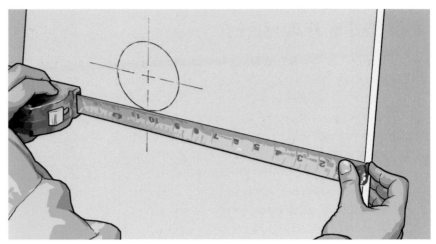

1 To mark for small pipes, use a T-square and the coordinate method for locating the center of the pipe's precise location on the wall, which you can then transfer to the drywall panel.

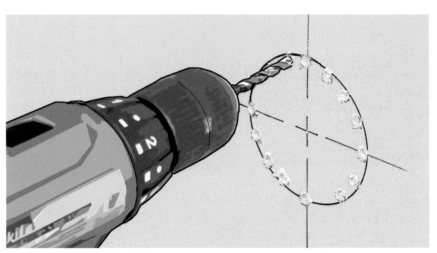

2 To cut out a hole in cement-based tile backer board, locate and mark the pipe's position. Then use a drill with a ⅛-in. masonry bit to drill holes in the drywall around the pipe's outline.

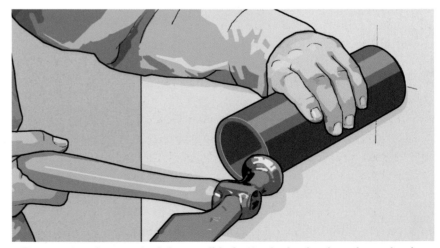

3 Once you have poked the small holes in the backer-board panel, take your section of discarded pipe and drive it through the panel. The resulting hole should be a perfect fit for the pipe in question.

USING A STEP-UP BENCH

BY MODIFYING A SAWHORSE with a wide top plank and side rails that serve as steps, you can create a handy step-up bench that works well for many drywalling tasks. Simply add a 2×10 plank to the top and two 2×4 or 1×6 side rails as shown in the illustration. You can also rent or buy sawhorses, step-up benches, or trestles that are designed for drywall installation.

Work Trestle. A step-up bench, or work trestle, provides a handy combination short stepladder and work platform for many drywall applications. The height of the trestle should be determined by subtracting your own height from the overall height of the room.

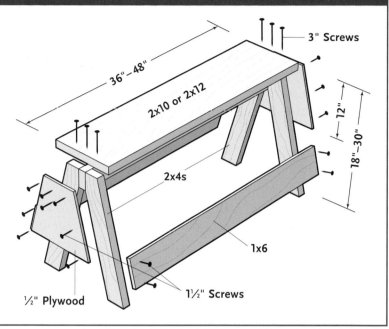

3" Screws

36"–48"

2×10 or 2×12

12"

18"–30"

2×4s

1×6

½" Plywood

1½" Screws

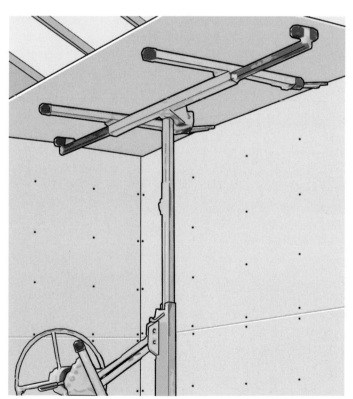

Panel Lifter. A panel jack, above, is a real work-saving device when drywalling ceilings. By mounting a panel and lifting it up into position, you have a nearly effortless way to provide ceiling-panel installation.

Stilts. Shoe stilts take some getting used to, right, and they can be awkward and dangerous. When mastered, they can provide high access and mobility for finishing drywall.

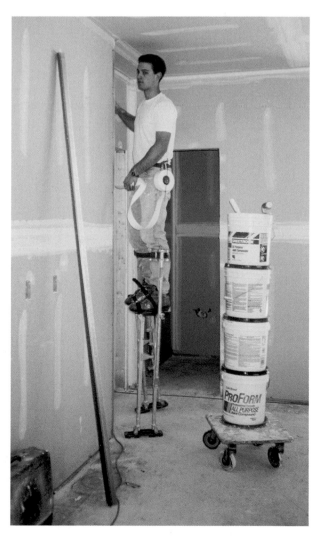

FASTENING DRYWALL

For a number of reasons, screws have replaced nails as the dominant fastener used to attach drywall to framing or existing walls. First, you can remove them, in case you should have to pull off a panel for trimming. It's also easier to control a screw's depth, and screwdriving doesn't knock furring strips or studs out of alignment, as hammering does. Screws install more quickly than nails, especially with a self-loading screw gun. Finally, screws simply offer more holding power than nails.

Whether you go with screws or nails, there are three types of each to choose from. (See page 20.) Select Type W screws if you're fastening drywall to wood studs or furring, Type G screws to attach drywall to drywall in a two-layer application, and Type S self-drilling screws if you're fastening drywall to metal studs.

Ringed nails, which have 25 percent more holding power than smooth-shank nails, are used to fasten drywall to wood. Cement-coated nails make use of their coating to add holding power. Cooler nails are used for hanging drywall over rigid insulation.

FASTENING DRYWALL WITH NAILS

DRIVE NAILS WITH A DRYWALL HAMMER, which has a face that leaves a dimple. When nailing, work across either the length or width of the panel, applying the full schedule of nails as you proceed with each row. Don't nail the perimeter and then the interior. As you work, hold the drywall panel flush against the furring or studs. Don't expect the final hammer blows to miraculously drive the panel tight against the framing.

Keep at least a ⅜-inch margin between the edge of the wallboard and each nail. If you're not using an adhesive, position nails 7 inches apart on ceiling panels and 8 inches apart on wall panels. With an adhesive, you can space them every 16 inches or so on ceilings or walls.

When fully driven, the nailhead should sit in a dimple about 1/32 inch deep but shouldn't tear the face paper. Make this dimple with the last blow of the hammer. (If you're having trouble with nails popping out, you can try double-nailing the panels instead. See "Fixing Popped Nails or Screws," pages 128–129.)

No Adhesive. Drywall attached to framing using nails but no adhesive requires a maximum 7-in.-on-center fastener spacing on ceilings and a maximum 8-in.-on-center fastener spacing on walls.

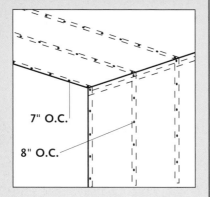

7" O.C.

8" O.C.

Adhesive. Drywall attached to framing with nails and heavy-duty construction adhesive reduces the requirement to a maximum 16-in.-on-center fastener spacing on both ceilings and walls.

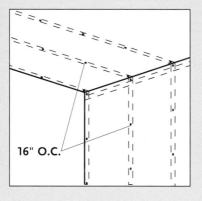

16" O.C.

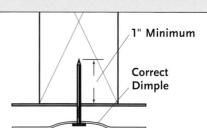

1" Minimum

Correct Dimple

Good. A well-driven nail leaves the paper face undamaged and has the best holding power.

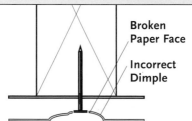

Broken Paper Face

Incorrect Dimple

Bad. An improperly driven nail, which has torn the face paper, offers little holding power.

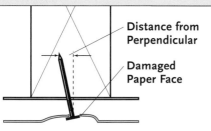

Distance from Perpendicular

Damaged Paper Face

Bad. This nail, driven at an angle, still shows damage to the face, creating a weakened connection.

FASTENING DRYWALL WITH SCREWS

DRIVE SCREWS with a variable-speed drill and Phillips-head driver, or use a self-feeding screw gun. As with nails, work across the length or width of the panel. Never screw the entire perimeter and then the interior.

As you work, hold the panel flush against the framing. If there is a gap between the drywall and the studs, the screw will sink through the panel instead of drawing it tight against the studs.

Again, keep each screw at least ⅜ inch in from the edge of the panel. Position screws along each edge and each framing member, spacing them every 12 inches for ceilings and 16 inches for walls.

When using adhesives on ceilings in which the panels lie parallel with the joists, apply screws every 16 inches along the edges and 24 inches along frame members.

If the panels lie perpendicular to framing, apply screws every 16 inches on the ends and edges and either 16 or 24 inches on the interior, depending on the frame spacing.

When using adhesives in wall applications, space screws (both horizontally and vertically) to match the stud spacing, whether the panels lie perpendicular or parallel to the framing.

If possible, drive drywall screws using a screw gun with an adjustable clutch. The clutch can be set to drive the screw to the appropriate depth, at which point it will disengage.

Make sure that you drive screws squarely into the panels. Driving them at an angle will tear the paper, which makes finishing more difficult, reduces the screws' holding power, and limits the sheer strength of the panel.

Screws vs. Nails. Screws offer more holding power than nails, but skilled use of the drywall hammer still has its place.

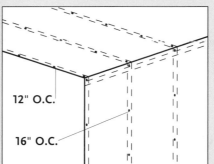

No Adhesive. Drywall screwed to framing without adhesives demands a maximum 12-in.-on-center fastener spacing on ceilings and a maximum 16-in.-OC fastener spacing on walls.

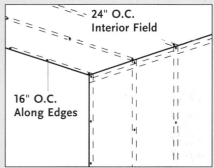

Adhesive. Drywall screwed to ceilings (parallel with the joists) with adhesive demands a maximum 16-in.-OC spacing on the edges and 24-in.-OC interior spacing.

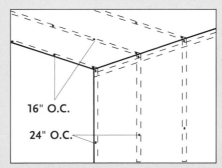

Adhesive. Drywall screwed to ceilings (perpendicular to the joists) framed 16 in. OC with adhesive demands a maximum 16-in.-OC fastener spacing. Drywall screwed to walls framed 16 in. OC with adhesives demands a maximum 24-in.-OC fastener spacing.

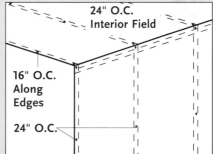

Adhesive. Drywall screwed to ceilings framed 24 in. OC with adhesive demands a maximum 16-in.-OC fastener spacing along edges and a 24-in.-OC spacing in its interior. Drywall screwed to walls framed 24 in. OC with adhesive demands a maximum 24-in.-OC fastener spacing.

HANGING DRYWALL ON A CEILING

A ceiling installation generally requires two people, preferably three, and should always be done before the walls. With a three-person crew, two can hold the panel in place while the third drives the fasteners. If you have a two-person crew, both workers will hold the panel in place as they fasten.

One person can hang a ceiling, but it takes skill and patience. If you intend to try it, temporarily nail 2×4s on the top plates, leaving just enough space for the panels (½ inch, ⅝ inch, or whatever thickness you're using). Using these blocks and a deadman or two, you can probably handle the job solo if you can't find any helpers.

As with any drywall job, choose longer panel lengths to reduce the number of joints. Install the longest panel you can handle. If your ceiling measures 10 × 12 feet, use three 4 × 10-foot panels rather than three 8-foot panels (with patches to fill in the gaps). This will reduce the amount of finish work substantially. (See "Creating Layouts," pages 41–43, for solutions.)

Hanging Drywall on a Ceiling. Always take care not to hurt your neck or your lower back when hanging ceiling panels.

pro tip

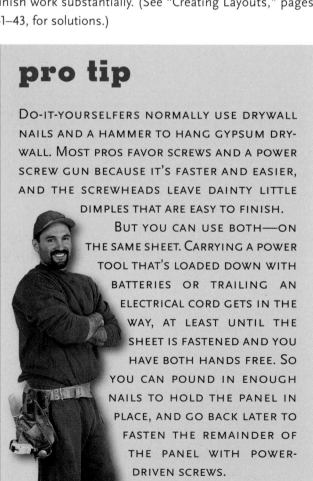

DO-IT-YOURSELFERS NORMALLY USE DRYWALL NAILS AND A HAMMER TO HANG GYPSUM DRYWALL. MOST PROS FAVOR SCREWS AND A POWER SCREW GUN BECAUSE IT'S FASTER AND EASIER, AND THE SCREWHEADS LEAVE DAINTY LITTLE DIMPLES THAT ARE EASY TO FINISH.

BUT YOU CAN USE BOTH—ON THE SAME SHEET. CARRYING A POWER TOOL THAT'S LOADED DOWN WITH BATTERIES OR TRAILING AN ELECTRICAL CORD GETS IN THE WAY, AT LEAST UNTIL THE SHEET IS FASTENED AND YOU HAVE BOTH HANDS FREE. SO YOU CAN POUND IN ENOUGH NAILS TO HOLD THE PANEL IN PLACE, AND GO BACK LATER TO FASTEN THE REMAINDER OF THE PANEL WITH POWER-DRIVEN SCREWS.

FASTENING EDGES

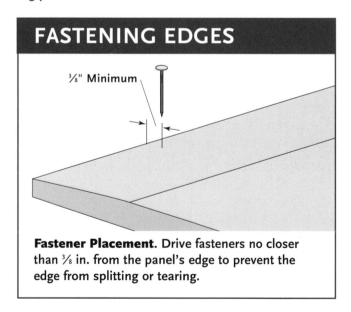

⅜" Minimum

Fastener Placement. Drive fasteners no closer than ⅜ in. from the panel's edge to prevent the edge from splitting or tearing.

Wrong

Correct

Driving Screws. An overdriven drywall screw has torn the panel's face paper, left. A properly driven screw, right, has its head sitting just beneath the drywall's face.

Hanging Drywall on a Ceiling

Difficulty Level:

TOOLS & MATERIALS
- Drywall panels ▪ Measuring tape
- Utility knife ▪ Permanent marker
- Sawhorses and planks or scaffolding
- Caulking gun and drywall adhesive
- Screw gun ▪ Drywall screws (or nails)

1 **Make the necessary cuts on the drywall, and mark the joists.** Cut a drywall panel to size, and then cut holes for utility boxes, pipes, and ductwork, as explained in Chapter 4, beginning on page 64. After cutting, mark the joist locations on the top plate with a permanent marker so that you'll be able to find them after you've positioned the panel. Rest the panel so that the face side will face downward when it is picked up and put in place against the ceiling joists or furring. Position your scaffold or sawhorses and planks parallel with the long edge of the panel (generally, perpendicular to the joists). This will provide solid footing and a sturdy work surface along the full length of the panel.

Apply adhesive to the studs. If required, apply adhesive to the joists or furring. Even if you have two workers, you may want to nail 2×4s to the top plate (as recommended on page 84 for solo installation).

2 **Position the FIRST panel.** With a helper, pick up the panel, and tuck one side into the corner where the ceiling and wall meet. With this end of the panel positioned, push the other end into place. If it binds, the panel needs to be trimmed—don't force it. If the panel fits properly, move on to Step 3.

3 **Fasten the panel in place.** With the panel in position, hold it flush against the furring or joists. (Two workers can support it with their heads. However, this can put a kink in your neck, particularly if you turn from side to side under the panel's weight. To ease the strain, keep movements to a minimum, and remove the head support once you've driven six or seven fasteners.) Fasten the panel in place using screws or nails, following the schedules presented earlier in this chapter. Continue toward the opposite corner in this way, butting each new panel tight against the previous one.

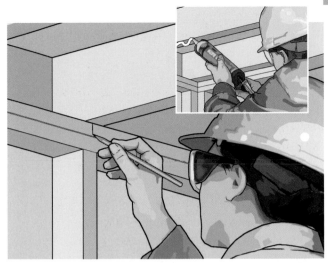

1 The location of the ceiling joists should be marked on the top plate, so they can be easily found after the panel is lifted into place. Apply adhesive (insert) to each joist to be covered by the panel.

2 Two people can easily move the ceiling panel into position, but have fasteners ready once the panel is snug against the joists.

3 Keeping the panel tight against the joists, attach nails or screws according to the ceiling fastener schedule.

Installing Drywall

HANGING DRYWALL ON A FLAT WALL

Attaching panels to a flat wall goes more quickly than installing them on a ceiling. However, lifting and positioning the top row still takes a good deal of energy and planning. It's only when you get to the bottom row that the job becomes relatively easy. Whether you're covering a ceiling or a wall, the same principles apply:

- Install the largest panel you can handle.
- Hold the panel firmly against the framing before fastening it in place.
- When sizing a panel, cut it small enough to fit without binding but large enough that it doesn't leave a gap too wide (more than about ¼ inch) to be taped and filled easily.

Hanging Drywall. Two people can attach drywall panels to a flat wall, right, with the greatest of ease.

pro tip

WITH A CREW OF THREE, LET THE DRYWALL CUTTER START A ROW OF NAILS ALONG THE EDGE OF THE SHEETS THAT WILL BUTT AGAINST THE CEILING BEFORE THEY ARE FITTED INTO PLACE. THE SHEETS ARRIVE IN PLACE READY FOR A QUICK HAMMERING, AND EVERYONE HOLDING THE SHEET CAN LET GO. IT WORKS WELL ALONG THE CEILING, WHERE THE CUTTER DOESN'T HAVE TO MEASURE 16-INCH CENTERS TO START THE NAILS OVER STUDS. A ROUGH ESTIMATE IS FINE BECAUSE OF THE DOUBLE 2x4 PLATE THAT'S USUALLY ABOVE THE STUDS.

Installing Drywall

Hanging Drywall on a Flat Wall

Difficulty Level:

TOOLS & MATERIALS
▪ Drywall panels ▪ Measuring tape ▪ Utility knife
▪ Adhesive and caulking gun ▪ Screw gun
▪ Drywall screws (or nails) ▪ Panel lifter

1 **Prepare the panel, and apply adhesive.** Cut a drywall panel to size, and then cut holes for utility boxes, pipes, and ductwork, as explained in Chapter 4, beginning on page 64. Rest the panel so that the face side will face outward when you pick it up and position it on the wall. If required, apply adhesive to studs or furring.

2 **Place the panel on the wall.** As a general rule, hang the top row first. With a helper, pick up the panel, and place it firmly against the stud wall. Check to see that the drywall covers just half of a stud face it will share with another panel. If necessary, rest an upper panel on nails driven into the studs until you secure it in place.

3 **Fasten the drywall to the studs.** Apply pressure to the panel to ensure full contact with framing members, and then screw or nail it in place using the schedules presented earlier in this chapter. (See pages 82–83.)

4 **Butt the lower panel upward.** Once you've installed the top row of drywall panels against the ceiling, push the lower rows of panels against them using some type of panel lifter. Remember, it's perfectly okay to leave a gap along the bottom at floor level—base molding will cover it.

1 After cutting the panel to size, apply construction adhesive to the face of studs with a caulking gun.

2 Wall panels should be raised upward, against the ceiling or the wall panel above it.

3 The drywall panel should be pressed firmly against the studs before attaching nails or screws. Drive two nails into the bottom edge to hold the panel in position.

4 A pry bar and block (or panel lifter) is an ideal tool for fine-tuning panel elevation on the floor level.

HANGING CORNERS & ANGLES

Hanging Drywall at an Inside Corner

Drywall panels can meet at an inside corner (either wall to wall or wall to ceiling) or an outside corner.

At inside corners, framing members must provide a nailing surface for drywall panels that meet there. The illustrations at upper right show two common variations: one for a true corner (where main walls meet) and one for a midwall corner (where a partition wall joins a main wall).

Once you cut the drywall to size and position it, you screw or nail it to the framing in the same manner, regardless of the type of studs used. The fact that a drywall edge meets in an inside corner does not change its fastener treatment, unless you want to create a floating corner. (See "Creating a Floating Wall Corner," page 92.)

Hanging Corners and Angles. Inside corners need to have a nailing base for both panels as part of the framing; otherwise, blocking or drywall clips must be added.

TYPES OF CORNER FRAMING

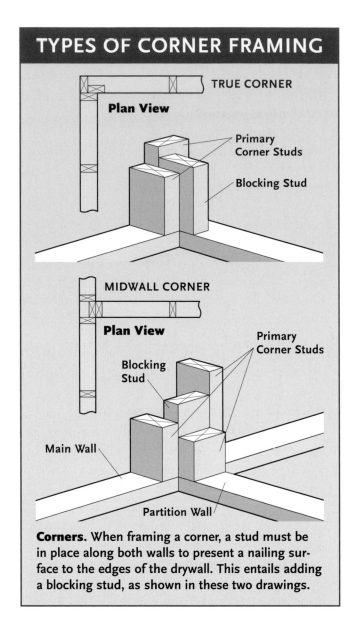

TRUE CORNER

Plan View

Primary Corner Studs

Blocking Stud

MIDWALL CORNER

Plan View

Primary Corner Studs

Blocking Stud

Main Wall

Partition Wall

Corners. When framing a corner, a stud must be in place along both walls to present a nailing surface to the edges of the drywall. This entails adding a blocking stud, as shown in these two drawings.

ANOTHER CORNER OPTION

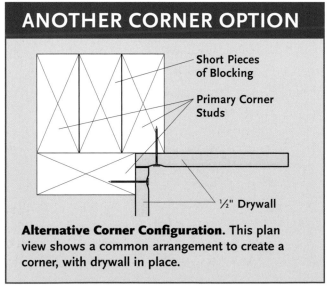

Short Pieces of Blocking

Primary Corner Studs

½" Drywall

Alternative Corner Configuration. This plan view shows a common arrangement to create a corner, with drywall in place.

USING DRYWALL CLIPS

OCCASIONALLY, you'll find an inside corner that is not framed in such a way that it presents a nailing surface. Nevertheless, panels meeting at corners must have a solid backing, so you'll need to install an extra stud. In cases where this is impossible, you can install drywall clips. These metal 90-degree angles have raised points on one face that are driven into the stud. To attach panels to the clips, use Type S drywall screws, driving them through both the drywall and the clip face.

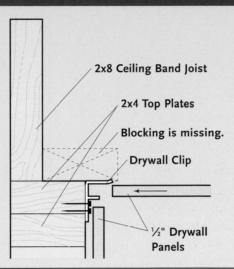

2x8 Ceiling Band Joist

2x4 Top Plates

Blocking is missing.

Drywall Clip

½" Drywall Panels

Drywall Clips. In the absence of a 2x4 nailer, use drywall clips. They can offer adequate support. In the example to the left, set the clip flush to the top of the upper top plate using drywall nails. Install the ceiling panel first as you normally would.

USING J-BEAD ON AN INSIDE CORNER

WHERE A DRYWALL PANEL MEETS a nondrywall surface on an inside corner, use J-bead to finish the edge. This metal or plastic angle has a lip along one edge that wraps around and covers the edge or end of the drywall panel. J-bead comes in either a finishing type or a reveal type. Make sure you match the J-bead size to your drywall thickness: ⅜-inch J-bead for ⅜-inch panels, and so on.

The finishing type resembles corner bead, in that you can finish it in place using joint compound. It has a raised bead that guides the finishing knife as it smooths a layer of joint compound over the exposed lip. You screw this type of J-bead in place before installing a panel in an inside corner. On an outside corner, fit the J-bead onto the drywall edge, and screw it in place after you've installed the panel.

The reveal type is meant to be left exposed. Its front lip has a finished face that presents a completed trim. You can screw this type in place before installing the panel, and then insert the drywall edge into the J-bead. Fasten the panel along its length, but don't screw or nail through the outer lip.

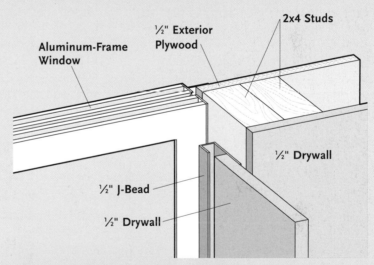

½" Exterior Plywood

2x4 Studs

Aluminum-Frame Window

½" Drywall

½" J-Bead

½" Drywall

J-bead. Trim pieces called J-bead are used to cover and finish the edge of a drywall panel that abuts a nondrywall surface.

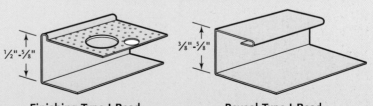

½"-⅝"

Finishing-Type J-Bead

⅜"-⅝"

Reveal-Type J-Bead

Two Types of J-bead. Finishing-type J-bead (above left) has a front flange designed to be finished using joint compound. The flange on the reveal-type J-bead (above right) is meant to be left exposed and requires no finishing.

Installing Drywall

USING L-BEAD

L-BEAD PROVIDES an edge treatment in areas where a drywall panel abuts nondrywall paneling, wood trim, or a door or window casing. As its name implies, L-bead has one face that is slightly wider than the other.

To install L-bead, first screw or nail the drywall in place, leaving a ⅛-inch reveal along its leading edge (the one that meets the non-drywall surface). Next, lay the L-bead in place with the finished face covering the leading edge and the perforated face resting on the drywall surface. Screw or nail the perforated face every 5 or 6 inches, and then cover it with joint compound. You don't have to tape this edge treatment, but it needs three coats of joint compound.

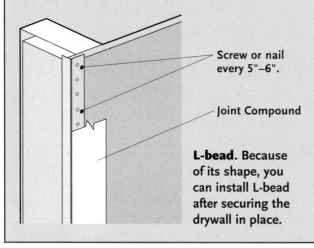

Screw or nail every 5"–6".

Joint Compound

L-bead. Because of its shape, you can install L-bead after securing the drywall in place.

HANGING OUTSIDE CORNERS

ON WALLS THAT FORM an outside corner, install one panel flush with the outside edge of the corner stud. Attach the adjoining panel so that it overlaps the edge of the first, creating a clean, square corner.

All outside corners require a corner bead, which is screwed in place and then finished with joint compound. Attach the bead with nails spaced every 5 or 6 inches, or set it in place with a corner crimper. Use the proper flange width for your drywall: 1¼ inch for ⅜-inch panels or 1⅛ inch for anything thinner. For half-height partition walls, box in the top of the stud wall with a piece of drywall that overlaps the two side panels. Then attach the corner bead, and finish it with joint compound.

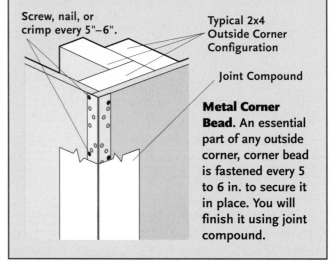

Screw, nail, or crimp every 5"–6".

Typical 2x4 Outside Corner Configuration

Joint Compound

Metal Corner Bead. An essential part of any outside corner, corner bead is fastened every 5 to 6 in. to secure it in place. You will finish it using joint compound.

USING J-BEAD ON AN OUTSIDE CORNER

WHERE A DRYWALL PANEL FORMS an outside corner that requires trim, J-bead can be used to create a clean edge. In this case, you friction-fit the J-bead onto the drywall edge before installation. Once you've positioned the panel, drive screws or nails through the J-bead and panel (or panel and J-bead if you're using reveal-type J-bead) into the stud.

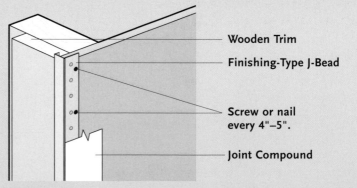

Wooden Trim

Finishing-Type J-Bead

Screw or nail every 4"–5".

Joint Compound

Outside-Corner J-bead. Apply finishing-type J-bead to the edge of drywall ending in an outside corner before installing it.

Creating a Sculptured Effect

Difficulty Level:

TOOLS & MATERIALS
▌ Drywall panels
▌ Measuring tape
▌ Chalk-line box
▌ Utility knife or saw
▌ Caulking gun
▌ Adhesive
▌ Laminating screws
▌ Special corner tape
▌ Joint compound

You can create sculptural reliefs (geometric or free-form) on walls and ceilings using layers of drywall. Fasten the drywall using adhesive and laminating screws.

1 Lay out the relief area. Using a chalk line for geometric areas or a pencil for free-form shapes, define the area you want to laminate. You can create stepped soffits on ceilings or decorative areas on walls.

2 Install the panels. Cut the shapes out using a utility knife or saw. Apply adhesive, and attach them with laminating screws.

3 Cover the edges. Apply flexible corner tape (available from drywall manufacturers in thicknesses to match the drywall you're using), and finish with joint compound. (See "Taping an Outside Corner," page 114.)

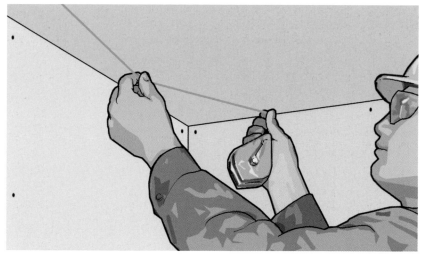

1 Mark out the area you want to laminate on the ceiling or wall. For straight designs, use a chalk line or straightedge and pencil.

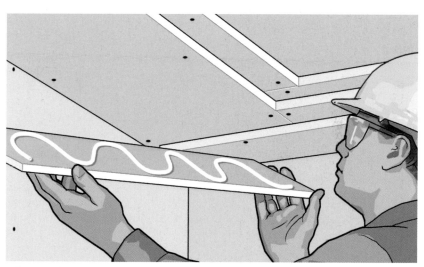

2 Cut drywall to the shape and size you need using a utility knife. Secure the pieces in layers using adhesive and laminating screws.

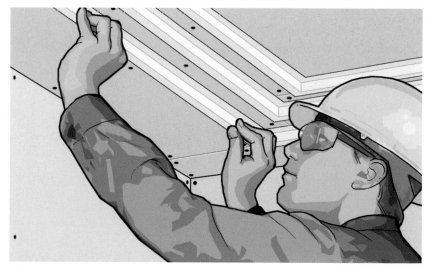

3 Create sharp edges using flexible corner tape and joint compound. The tape comes in sizes to fit different thicknesses of drywall.

Installing Drywall

Creating a Floating Wall Corner

Difficulty Level: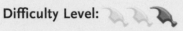

TOOLS & MATERIALS
▪ Basic hand tools ▪ Drywall panels
▪ Measuring tape ▪ Chalk-line box
▪ Utility knife ▪ Screw gun
▪ Sawhorses or scaffolding
▪ Drywall screws or nails

Because corner junctures are the first to *deflect* (the engineer's term for structural movement) as a building adjusts to moisture levels in the framing or to loads added to the structure, the drywall joints are the first to crack. Ironically, proper attachment of drywall with the full complement of screws or nails only aggravates the cracking. The more thoroughly the panels are attached, the more likely they are to move, crack, and gap along with the framing.

To ease this problem, avoid fastening one of the two drywall panels along the juncture. This solution, known as a floating corner, calls for no fasteners within 7 or 8 inches of the corner. The fastened panel holds the loose edge in place, allowing it to move and reducing the likelihood of cracking.

1 Install the first wall panel. Frame walls as you would on any standard corner, providing a nailing base for the edges of all panels. Install a panel in one corner, but fasten it only to within one stud bay of the inside edge. Don't fasten this edge to the corner stud.

2 Install the adjoining panel. On the adjoining wall, install the panel with a full schedule of screws or nails, trapping the first panel in place. Fasten this second panel to the corner stud as you would normally.

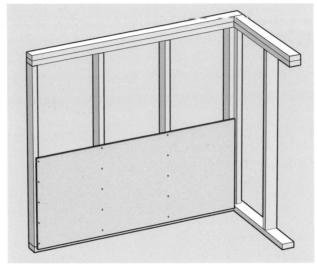

1 Fasten the first panel in the usual manner, but leave out the fasteners on the edge at the corner.

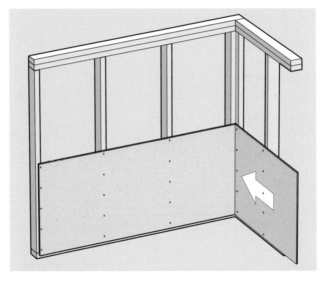

2 Fasten the second panel, trapping the unfastened corner of the first panel in place.

CORNER WALL CONFIGURATION

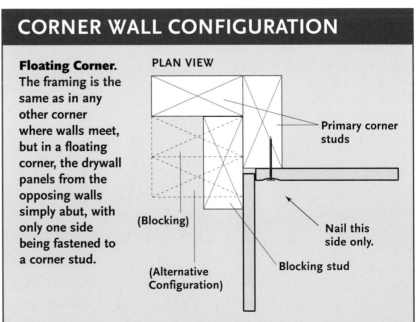

Floating Corner. The framing is the same as in any other corner where walls meet, but in a floating corner, the drywall panels from the opposing walls simply abut, with only one side being fastened to a corner stud.

PLAN VIEW
Primary corner studs
(Blocking)
Nail this side only.
(Alternative Configuration)
Blocking stud

Creating a Floating Corner in a Ceiling-Wall Joint

Difficulty Level:

TOOLS & MATERIALS
▮ Drywall panels ▮ Measuring tape
▮ Chalk-line box ▮ Utility knife
▮ Sawhorses and planks or scaffolding
▮ Screw gun ▮ Drywall screws

1 **Prepare the surface for installation.** Check the framing members of the wall and ceiling as you would for any standard drywalling job. Make sure to provide a nailing base for both the wall and ceiling panels by adding blocking or drywall clips where necessary.

2 **Install the ceiling panel.** Install a ceiling panel in the corner, but fasten it only to within 7 inches of the corner. Do not use any fasteners on the edge adjacent to the wall.

3 **Install the wall panel.** Install the adjoining wall panel, butting it against the ceiling panel as tightly as possible. Fasten it only to within 8 inches of the ceiling corner. The wall panel will trap the ceiling panel in place. Finish the floating joint as you would a normal joint.

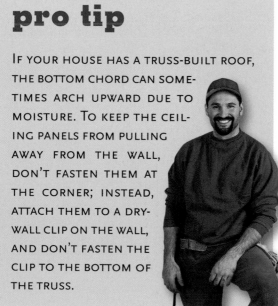

pro tip

IF YOUR HOUSE HAS A TRUSS-BUILT ROOF, THE BOTTOM CHORD CAN SOMETIMES ARCH UPWARD DUE TO MOISTURE. TO KEEP THE CEILING PANELS FROM PULLING AWAY FROM THE WALL, DON'T FASTEN THEM AT THE CORNER; INSTEAD, ATTACH THEM TO A DRYWALL CLIP ON THE WALL, AND DON'T FASTEN THE CLIP TO THE BOTTOM OF THE TRUSS.

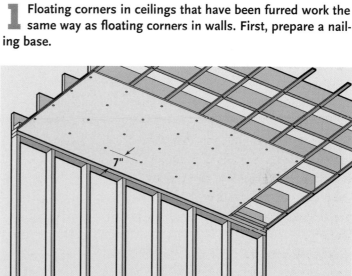

1 Floating corners in ceilings that have been furred work the same way as floating corners in walls. First, prepare a nailing base.

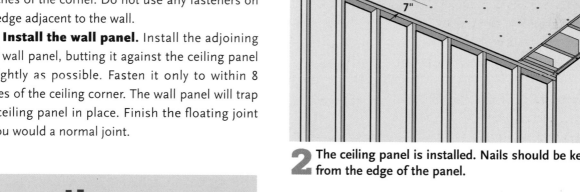

2 The ceiling panel is installed. Nails should be kept 7 in. from the edge of the panel.

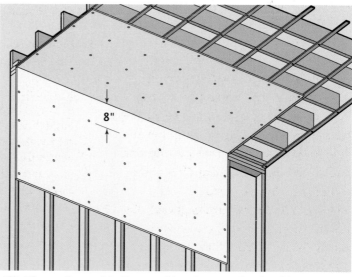

3 The wall panel is fastened in place. Nails should be kept 8 in. from the top edge of the panel.

INSTALLING DRYWALL ON STEEL FRAMING

Unlike wood, steel stud framing doesn't warp, shrink, or split. Termites and carpenter ants can't chew through it. It's much lighter than masonry, and it's easier and faster to assemble the pieces. It also won't rot, crumble, or add fuel to a fire. Because of all this, as well as its strength and durability—during a fire, for example, it can extend the time of possible escape before the walls collapse—steel framing is now the standard for commercial construction.

If steel offers so many advantages, why is it used in only 3 to 5 percent of residential building frames? For one thing, steel is a lot less accommodating than wood, which can often be coaxed and nudged into proper position. Steel construction also requires tools and skills quite different (though not necessarily more complicated) than wood framing, which is a disadvantage for do-it-yourselfers.

STEEL-STUD WALL PLAN

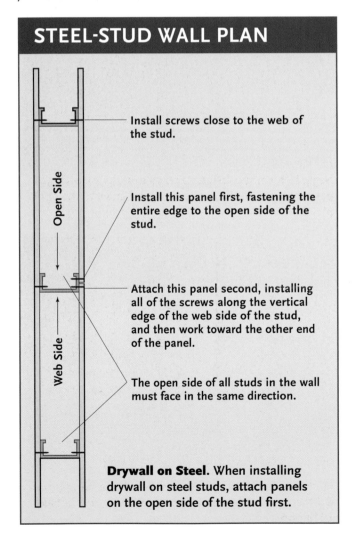

Install screws close to the web of the stud.

Install this panel first, fastening the entire edge to the open side of the stud.

Attach this panel second, installing all of the screws along the vertical edge of the web side of the stud, and then work toward the other end of the panel.

The open side of all studs in the wall must face in the same direction.

Drywall on Steel. When installing drywall on steel studs, attach panels on the open side of the stud first.

STEEL FRAMING MEMBERS

THE BASIC STEEL FRAMING MEMBER is three-sided; a 2x4 stud, for example, has two narrow 1¼- or 1½-inch edges (front and back) connected by only a single 3½- or 4-inch side, creating a shallow C-shape. Connectors are available in many shapes to join the framing members. Light-gauge steel thickness ranges from 12 to 25 gauge, with the lower numbers being thicker. The edges of framing members are usually rolled smooth during manufacturing, but they will become sharp when cut.

1 To begin the installation, snap a chalk line that is plumb with the soleplate, and screw a stud section to the framing above.

2 Nestle a stud into the channels of the soleplate and top plate, and clamp it in position before driving your screws.

3 To install a header, snip each edge of the header at a 45-deg. angle; bend the overage so that it tucks around the stud.

Installing Drywall on a Steel-Framed Wall

Difficulty Level:

TOOLS & MATERIALS
- Drywall panels ▌ Measuring tape
- Chalk-line box ▌ Utility knife
- Sawhorses or scaffolding
- Screw gun
- Bugle-head self-tapping screws

Although it is still uncommon, more houses are being built with steel framing every year. Installing drywall on steel studs is somewhat different from the method for wooden framing. For more information about steel framing (such as how to add blocking), see "Steel Framing Systems" in Chapter 3, pages 58–59. Remember to use bugle-head Type S screws with self-tapping points to install the drywall—ordinary Type W screws can drill through the 20-gauge steel of non-load-bearing steel studs, but drilling them in will dig out a hole in the drywall larger than the head of the screw, creating finishing problems and unstable drywall.

1 Determine the stud orientation. The open side of the C-shaped steel studs should all be facing in the same direction. You should install the drywall along a wall toward the open side of these channels. If you install the panels in the opposite direction—to the solid side first and then the open side—the open end may deflect outward, causing the panels to abut unevenly.

2 Install the first panel. Install the first wall panel in a corner, as you would for regular wood-framed installation. Begin fastening the screws at the edge away from the corner. At this edge, the screws should be driven in closer to the open side of the stud to allow for the adjacent panel to be installed. In the middle of the panel, drive screws as close to the solid side of the stud as possible, using the Type S screw schedule on page 83.

3 Install the next panel. Next, attach the abutting panel, and fasten the screws in the same way: starting at the far edge and then working your way back to the joint.

1 Drywall must be installed toward the open side of the steel studs. Check the spacing to ensure panels will have backing.

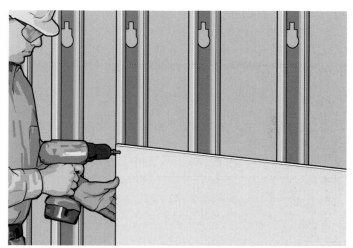

2 Begin in a corner, fastening screws on the side of the panel away from the corner first, and close to the open part of the stud.

3 Abut the next panel, and fasten it in the same way you did the previous panel: far end first. Here, the installer is finishing up.

HANGING DRYWALL IN TRICKY LOCATIONS

Hanging a Curved Wall

Difficulty Level: 🔧🔧🔧

TOOLS & MATERIALS
- Measuring tape ▪ Drywall panels ▪ Plant mister
- Water (a quart for every 4 x 8 drywall panel)
- Utility knife ▪ Sawhorses or scaffolding
- Screw gun ▪ Drywall screws

Curved walls usually are hung with flexible ¼-inch-thick panels that are designed specifically for such applications (and thus require no special preparation). As an alternative, you can dampen or slit thicker panels as directed in Step 2. Curved walls require horizontal installation of panels. For dampened panels, you should avoid cutting out for utilities until the panel has been installed and allowed to dry thoroughly (24 hours). (Mark their location on the floor, and note their heights and dimensions.)

Before you think about hanging panels, you'll probably need to add additional studs. Curved drywall installation requires closer spacing than the 16- or 24-inch on-center in a typical flat wall. For ¼-inch panels, space the studs no more than 6 inches apart; for ⅜-inch, go with a maximum of 8 inches; and for ½-inch stock, stick with 12 inches. (Avoid ⅝-inch drywall; it doesn't bend well.)

Note in the illustration below left that the inside and outside lengths of a curved wall are not the same. The outside, convex panel has to travel a slightly greater distance than the inside, concave panel. On either side, it's best to cover the curved section with a single panel, because finishing seams on curved walls makes for tedious work. Use over-long panels, and trim them to length after installation. If the curve measures 13 feet, for example, use a 14-foot panel. (You'll end up with slightly more excess on the concave, or inner, side; this makes little difference if you're trimming over-long panels to length, but it can throw you off if you're attempting to cover the curve with shorter pieces that must fit exactly.)

1 Check stud on-center spacing. Double-check the framing to make sure that the maximum stud-to-stud distance does not exceed the spacing recommended for your drywall thickness.

2 Wet down the drywall. (optional) Using a plant mister, spray a quart of water (for a full 4 × 8-foot panel) on the panel side that will be compressed (the face side for a concave wall; the back side for a convex wall). **Note:** Dampened panels can fall apart, so use at least two, preferably three, people to pick one up. Wait one hour before installation to give the water a chance to soak in.

3 Slit the back of the panel. (optional) As an alternative for concave walls, cut ⅛-inch deep kerf marks every 2 to 3 inches (or ¾ to 1½ inches for ½-inch drywall) in the back side of the panel. (For a very tight radius, it may be necessary to wet and slit the panel.)

4 Fasten the panel to the curve. Apply drywall adhesive to the stud edges. With at least one other person, install the drywall panel. Use 1¼-inch Type W screws rather than nails. For concave installation, start by screwing the panel to the center studs, and then work toward the end. On convex surfaces, start at one end of the panel, and work your way across.

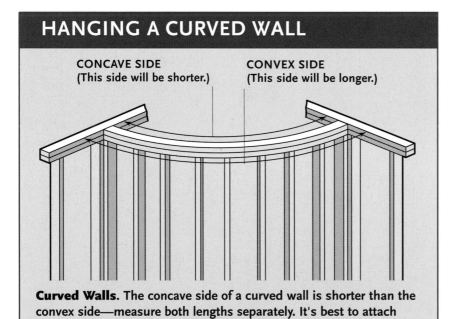

HANGING A CURVED WALL

CONCAVE SIDE
(This side will be shorter.)

CONVEX SIDE
(This side will be longer.)

Curved Walls. The concave side of a curved wall is shorter than the convex side—measure both lengths separately. It's best to attach overlong pieces when circumstances allow, and then cut them to size, as these distances are hard to measure.

1 Check stud spacing to provide proper support for drywall panels. For a single-layer application of ¼ in. drywall as shown here, studs should be no more than about 6 in. apart.

2 To bend conventional drywall, first mist it with water. A plant mister will serve well for this purpose. In this application, the face side of the drywall panel is being sprayed.

3 If necessary for a tight radius, slit the back of the drywall with a utility knife before bending it.

4 It takes at least two people to keep a formerly straight piece of drywall tight against a curved wall.

Installing Drywall

INSTALLING AN ARCHWAY

The underside of an archway is nothing more than a miniature curved ceiling. You drywall it in much the same way that you'd cover a curved wall, using ¼-inch-thick flexible drywall. This material has the flexibility to conform to a fairly small radius without cracking, and it doesn't require dampening or slitting. (If a single layer doesn't provide enough thickness for your wall design or doesn't come flush with the panels covering the wall, install two layers of it, one atop the other.)

If you can't obtain ¼-inch panels or don't want to buy a 4 × 8-foot sheet (often the smallest unit sold) for one small archway, you can use ½-inch-thick drywall. To use this on any but the gentlest of curves without cracking it during installation, you'll have to dampen the back side and slit it every ¾ to 1½ inches across the back, depending on the radius of your arch. (See "Hanging a Curved Wall," beginning on page 96.)

Once you cut the piece to the length and width of your archway, hold it in place, and start fastening it in the center. Then, alternating from side to side, work toward both ends of the piece, fastening it every 6 inches. Check for sags, and add fasteners where necessary. Finish the archway-to-wall joints with flexible vinyl corner bead.

Archways. Whether the top of a curved wall opening or a grandiose entryway, installing arched panels is a challenge.

Installing an Archway. Flexible ¼-in. panels should fit in an archway without cracking—if not, wet it down and try again.

BENDING RADII FOR DRYWALL

These bending radii consider the arc of the curved piece of drywall as part of a circle. (The larger the radius, the shallower the curve.) To estimate your bending radius, you'll have to extend your arc into a full circle (either by measuring or estimating) and then measure the radius from the center of the circle.

Formula for Determining the Radius from an Arc

$$2 \times A \times Y = A^2 + B^2$$

Height or Rise of Chord (A)

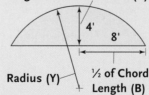

4'
8'

Radius (Y) ½ of Chord Length (B)

With some simple math you can easily calculate the radius of a circle. Plugging in the numbers from the example at the left:

$$2 \times 4 \times Y = 16 + 64$$
$$8Y = 80$$
$$Y \text{ (Radius)} = 10'$$

THICKNESS	DRY	WET	SPECIAL FLEX PANELS
¼-inch-thick	5' R.	2–3' R.	1½–3' R.
⅜-inch-thick	7½' R.	3–4' R.	n/a
½-inch-thick	20' R.	4–5' R.	n/a

Drywalling Stairway Walls

Difficulty Level:

TOOLS & MATERIALS
- Drywall panels ▪ Measuring tape
- Chalk-line box ▪ Utility knife ▪ 4-foot T-square
- Scaffolding or stepladder, planks, and clamps
- Screw gun ▪ Drywall screws (or nails)

Stairways present a challenge because they often have angled surfaces. You can simplify the job by installing as many full panels as possible and then measuring and installing the odd-shaped panels last. The existing full panels will give you two of the three dimensions for each triangular panel, which makes it easy to find the length of the third.

1 Cover the larger areas with drywall first. Install as many full panels as will fit on the stairway wall, using the same arrangement (horizontal or vertical) that you've used elsewhere.

2 Measure smaller, irregular shapes. With the full panels in place, measure for two of the three sides of each triangular piece that must be cut to fit. Transfer those dimensions onto a full panel using a 4-foot T-square.

3 Cut the triangular piece to fit. Once you've transferred the two known dimensions, snap a chalk line (or use a straightedge) to connect the end points and mark the unknown length with a cut line. Cut and install this partial panel as you would any other piece of drywall.

Tricky Shapes. Drywalling unusual shapes requires extra patience in measuring and cutting, but the hanging is the same.

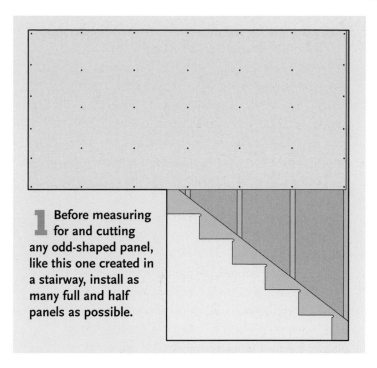

1 Before measuring for and cutting any odd-shaped panel, like this one created in a stairway, install as many full and half panels as possible.

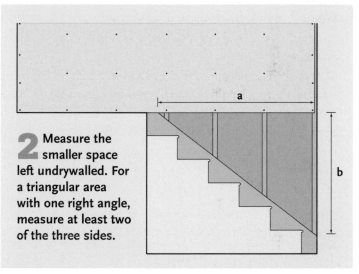

2 Measure the smaller space left undrywalled. For a triangular area with one right angle, measure at least two of the three sides.

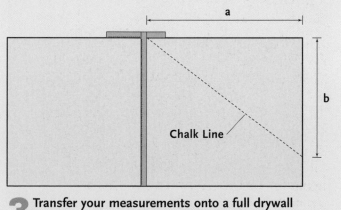

3 Transfer your measurements onto a full drywall panel, and cut out the irregular shape.

Installing Drywall

Drywalling Cathedral Ceilings

Difficulty Level: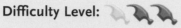

TOOLS & MATERIALS
▌Measuring tape ▌Chalk-line box
▌Drywall adhesive ▌Drywall panels
▌Utility knife ▌Drywall jack ▌Stepladder
▌Screw gun and drywall screws (or nails)

Install a cathedral ceiling as you would any other ceiling panel. Use adhesive for a better bond between the panels and rafters, and use the ceiling fastener schedule for nails or screws. Install each panel using a drywall jack, or have two workers stand on stepladders. You'll find that scaffolding is difficult to move around during cathedral-ceiling installation because the drywall jack tends to get in the way. However, scaffolding makes it much easier to finish these panels once you've installed them.

1 Apply adhesive to the bottom edge of the rafters where you'll be installing the panel.

2 When hanging a large cathedral ceiling, a panel lift and a tall sturdy stepladder are two essential tools in the absence of scaffolding. This is at least a two-person job, and it involves moving the stepladder if you are to fully secure the drywall with fasteners.

1 **Apply adhesive.** If necessary, apply adhesive to the rafter edges or furring. Be careful not to work too far ahead of yourself with the adhesive, as it can set up before you get to that section of ceiling.

2 **Raise the panel using a drywall jack.** Place a panel onto a drywall jack. As always, use the largest panel you can handle to minimize finishing work. Raise the jack until the panel makes snug contact with the rafters or furring.

3 **Fasten the panel to the ceiling.** Move a stepladder into place on one side of the drywall jack, being careful not to disturb its base. Working safely from a lower rung, adjust the angle of the jack as needed, making sure that the panel is tight against the framing members. Then fasten the panel to the ceiling using the screw or nail schedule recommended earlier. Work your way across the panel, getting as close to the jack as possible. Then move the ladder to the opposite side of the jack and continue fastening. Move the jack away from the wall only when the drywall is entirely fastened.

3 When fastening the panels to the ceiling, it's best to have a helper keep the drywall jack steady.

Drywalling Odd-Shaped Areas

Difficulty Level:

TOOLS & MATERIALS
▌ Measuring tape ▌ Chalk-line box
▌ Drywall panels ▌ 4-foot T-square ▌ Utility knife
▌ Stepladder ▌ Screw gun
▌ Drywall screws (or nails)

Every house seems to have an odd-shaped corner that can't be drywalled with squares, rectangles, or easy-to-figure triangles. The trick is to break down an odd shape into its component lengths or sides, then use a framing square or T-square to transfer the dimensions onto the wallboard. If possible, use a fresh corner or factory edge of the panel for reference in laying out such a piece.

1 **Measure the area.** Determine the dimensions and angles of the odd-shaped area.

2 **Mark the cuts on the panel.** Using a T-square, ruler, or framing square, transfer the dimensions onto a drywall panel. Try to use a factory edge for at least one side of the cutout piece.

3 **Make your cuts.** Cut out the piece using a utility knife. If you can't snap this piece cleanly from the panel, score the cut lines repeatedly with your utility knife to make a clean cut, or use a drywall saw.

4 **Install the piece.** Test-fit the piece in the odd-shaped hole. Trim its edges where necessary, and fasten it.

1 Measure each side of the area you want to fill. Drawing yourself a diagram of the shape is helpful.

2 Transfer the dimensions onto a piece of drywall, and incorporate the panel's factory edges if possible.

3 Cut out the piece with a sharp utility knife. Snap it back if you can, otherwise keep scoring until you break through.

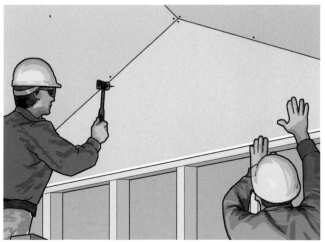

4 Install the drywall piece, and fasten it with at least two nails or screws along each edge, or—for larger panel pieces—the recommended on-center spacing.

Installing Drywall

Building a Drywall Box around Pipes and Utilities

Difficulty Level:

TOOLS & MATERIALS
▌ Measuring tape
▌ Basic hand tools
▌ Chalk-line box
▌ Power miter saw
▌ 2x4 or ¾x4 lumber
▌ Drywall panels
▌ Utility knife
▌ T-square
▌ Screw gun and drywall adhesive
▌ Screws or nails for framing and drywall

In some areas of the house (especially basements), you'll want to cover exposed pipes, utilities, or ductwork with drywall. However, drywall can't be attached directly to such fixtures, so you'll have to build a frame box to provide a nailing base for the panels.

1 Measure for your framing. Decide on the size of the box needed to cover the pipes or ductwork. Remember that the frame itself will make the drywall stand off the pipe or duct by at least 1½ inches. You may want to make a larger box for design purposes—one that would hold recessed lighting, say. Leave sufficient room for sound-attenuating, fireproof blanket insulation, which is required by many local building codes.

2 Build the framing. Frame around the duct or pipe, making sure that you provide a nailing base for all drywall edges. Use the same on-center spacing recommended earlier for walls. (This will vary according to the panel thickness you intend to use.) Install the insulation when the frame is completed.

3 Drywall the box. Cut and install drywall on the box framing. Use a ceiling screw or nail schedule for all horizontal sections and a wall schedule for the vertical panels. Complete the corners using corner bead.

1 To drywall over a duct, first measure the duct's dimensions.

Building a Drywall Box around Utilities or Pipes. Hiding ducts has a practical side, but the boxes can also be decorative.

102

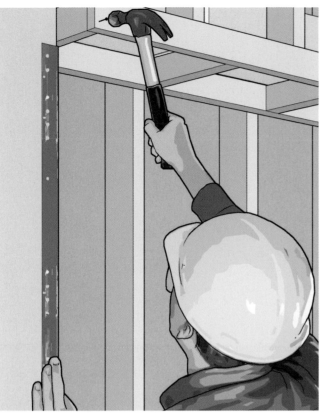

2 Frame in the duct with lumber so that the drywall will have a solid nailing or screwing base, as with a regular wall.

3 Attach drywall to the box frame with the same nail or screw schedules you use on walls. When the pipe or duct is boxed in, complete outside and inside corners.

DRYWALLING AROUND BEAMS AND POSTS

EVEN IF YOUR BASEMENT is unfinished you may want to conceal support beams and posts. In most cases you can build a frame around the obstacle to support the drywall.

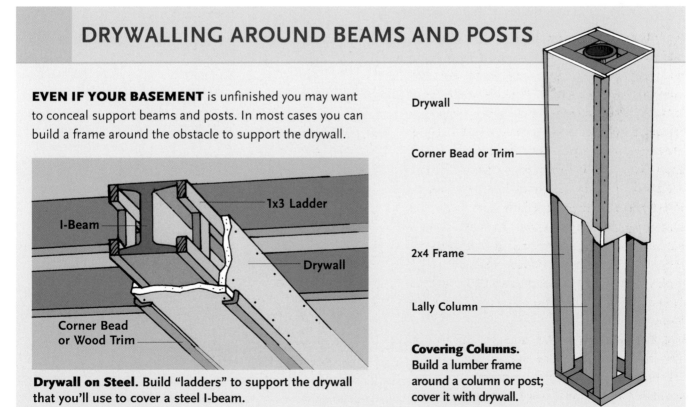

I-Beam

1x3 Ladder

Drywall

Corner Bead or Wood Trim

Drywall on Steel. Build "ladders" to support the drywall that you'll use to cover a steel I-beam.

Drywall

Corner Bead or Trim

2x4 Frame

Lally Column

Covering Columns.
Build a lumber frame around a column or post; cover it with drywall.

HANGING BACKER BOARD

The type of material required as backer board for tile depends on the tile's location and the type of adhesive you will use. If you're using an organic mastic adhesive and the area will not sustain consistent wetting, standard (or water-resistant) gypsum panels may serve the purpose. However, if the area will have to withstand regular soakings (a shower stall, sink surround, or kitchen-sink area), a cement-based backer board is required. This material also works well in dry areas that call for a heavy underlayment, such as a tiled half-wall surrounding a woodstove, where the surface must be fire-resistant.

- **Product choices:** Cementitious backer board, a portland cement-based product, comes in ½- and ⅝-inch thicknesses. You can purchase 4 × 8-foot stock, but panels typically measure 32 or 36 inches wide by 5 or 8 feet long.
- **Framing:** Framing for cement-based backer board must be spaced no more than 16 inches on center. Steel framing must be 20-gauge or heavier.
- **Vapor barrier:** Because tile can admit some water, a small percentage of which can then pass through the cement panels, the framing needs a vapor barrier to protect it from moisture. Attach 6-mil polyethylene sheeting as a barrier to the framing using a minimum overlap of 2 inches, or staple it to the back face of the panels using galvanized staples.
- **Fasteners:** Fasteners must be spaced more closely than with typical drywall (8 inches for walls, 6 inches

Hanging Backer Board for Tile. Cement-based panels protect the wall from water damage in bathrooms and kitchens.

for ceilings). You'll need special fasteners for cement-panel applications. Use 1½-inch 11-gauge galvanized roofing nails or 1¼-inch galvanized-steel screws. Do not use regular drywall nails or screws. These can rust through, causing the backer board to fail. (To estimate fastener quantities, figure on 1½ times the normal drywall-fastener requirement.)

- **Taping:** Cement-panel joints must be taped in a similar manner to those on regular drywall, although you don't need to finish the joints with trowels and sandpaper. Use tile-setting mortar or tile adhesive instead of joint compound. Tape the joints with a 2-inch-wide polymer-coated, fiberglass mesh tape that is specially designed for cement backer board.

INSTALLING BACKER BOARD

ALTHOUGH USED AS A SUBSTITUTE for drywall in wet locations, cement backer board is installed in much the same way as drywall. Cut the material using a utility knife, and attach to framing with galvanized fasteners. Use mesh tape on seams between panels.

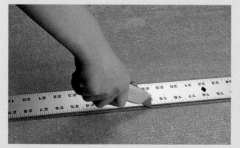

Cutting. Cut backer board the same way you cut drywall: score it using a utility knife; snap it along the score line.

Attaching. Nail backer boards up using galvanized roofing nails, or screw then in place using galvanized screws.

Installing Backer Board

Difficulty Level:

TOOLS & MATERIALS

▮ Vapor barrier (6-mil polyethylene sheeting)
▮ Staple gun with galvanized staples
▮ Measuring tape ▮ Cement-based backer board
▮ 4-foot T-square ▮ Utility knife ▮ Screw gun
▮ 1¼-inch galvanized-steel screws or 1½-inch galvanized roof nails
▮ 6- or 10-inch taping knife ▮ Tile mortar or adhesive
▮ 2-inch open-mesh polymer-coated tape

1 Install a vapor barrier. Fasten the 6-mil polyethylene vapor barrier over the 16-inch-on-center studs. Use galvanized roofing nails or a staple gun with galvanized staples.

2 Cut and install backer board. After cutting the cement-based backer board with a utility knife, fasten panels to the studs over the vapor barrier. Space the fasteners 8 inches apart on walls and 6 inches apart on ceilings.

3 Finish the joints. Using tile mortar or adhesive, fill and tape the joints where the backer-board panels meet. Apply a layer of tile mortar, embed the fiberglass mesh tape, and then follow with a wide knife to level the mortar.

1 Before you install backer board for tile, you'll need to put up a 6-mil polyethylene vapor barrier on the stud wall to keep the moisture inside the room from getting inside the wall cavity.

2 Install backer board with nails or screws 8 in. on center for walls, 6 in. on center for ceilings.

3 Using tile mortar or adhesive, fill and tape the joints where the backer-board panels meet. Bed the fiberglass mesh tape in a layer of tile mortar or adhesive, and finish using a wide knife.

6 taping & finishing

IN ANY DRYWALL JOB, taping and applying joint compound account for the lion's share of time. However, this part of the work can also yield the most satisfaction. After the hard work of installing drywall panels, the final appearance of the job really depends on how well you apply and finish off joint compound. It takes practice to tape and finish both quickly and neatly, but within a day or so, you'll find that your technique has developed pretty well. Before long, your work will compare favorably with that of the pros.

BASIC FINISHES

DURING OTHER PHASES OF THE JOB, drywallers rely on specialty tools to streamline the work. Taping and finishing, however, still call for the same tools that have been around since gypsum drywall was first introduced: wide knives for applying the joint compound and sandpaper for smoothing the joint after it has dried.

Taping joints involves four steps and requires three coats of joint compound. After you've installed and properly fastened the drywall, a rough coat (or tape-embedding coat) goes on first. While this coat is still wet, you press drywall tape into it, and then wipe away the excess joint compound. After this coat has dried, you apply a filler coat over the rough-coated tape, allow it to dry, and then use a wide knife to scrape high spots. Finally, a third coat (the finish coat) covers the entire joint. Once you've smoothed it a bit and feathered the edges, this coat should render the joint invisible beneath a coat of paint.

TAPING PREP: A CHECKLIST

- Ventilate the room with fans or by allowing a cross-breeze. This will lower humidity and accelerate the drying process.
- Double-check all panels to make sure that they're firmly attached.
- Verify that cutouts have been made for all outlets, switches, and fixtures.
- Assemble tools, joint compound, and tape in one area. Double-check estimates to ensure that you have sufficient joint compound and tape.
- Prefill any gap over ¼ inch wide with setting-type joint compound, and then smooth the face of the compound flush with the drywall face. Let this dry entirely before you start the taping procedure, and if necessary, scrape off any high spots.
- Clean and remove grit from all taping knives and trowels. Sand their faces smooth if necessary.
- Position ladders and scaffolds within easy reach.
- Make sure the temperature in the room where you'll apply joint compound remains at least 55 degrees F for 24 hours following application.

Prepare for Taping. The results of a perfect taping job should be invisible—the seams should be taped and sanded so that no ridges or humps can be seen on the painted wall.

pro tip

BEFORE USING JOINT COMPOUND, LOOSEN IT UP BY BLENDING IT WITH A MASHER. WELL-BLENDED JOINT COMPOUND GOES ON SMOOTHLY AND—IF MIXED CORRECTLY—SHOULDN'T CONTAIN LUMPS. ON THE OTHER HAND, JOINT COMPOUND THAT HAS BEEN OVERMIXED WILL BE FULL OF AIR BUBBLES, WHICH WILL POP AND SHOW UP AS LITTLE INDENTATIONS WHEN THE MUD DRIES. IN EITHER CASE, THE ONLY FIX IS TO SMOOTH DOWN THE MISTAKE, AND START AGAIN WITH A NEW BATCH OF MUD.

Taping & Finishing

Taping Joints on a Flat Wall

Difficulty Level: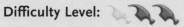

TOOLS & MATERIALS
▌ Drywall hawk or mud tray ▌ Joint compound
▌ 5- or 6-inch knife ▌ Drywall joint tape
▌ 10- or 12-inch straight-handled knife
▌ 10- or 12-inch beveled trowel
▌ 120-grit sandpaper or sanding sponge

1 Apply the first coat. Using a 5- or 6-inch knife, apply a coat of joint compound to the joints, spreading it evenly to a thickness of about ¼ inch. Cover the entire length of the joint. Fill any gaps between panels. **NOTE:** if you're using fiberglass mesh tape, apply it before the first coat. The compound then oozes through the mesh and binds to the wall.

2 Tape over the first coat. Working with a strip of drywall tape the same length as the entire joint, press the tape into the wet first coat using your fingers, being careful not to create any wrinkles. Make sure that the tape centers on the joint. Using a 5- or 6-inch knife (working from top to bottom on a vertical joint), apply light pressure to the tape, and draw the knife along its full length, squeezing joint compound out from beneath the tape as you smooth the coat. If the tape blisters, you haven't left enough joint compound beneath it. Peel the tape back in that section; add joint compound; and proceed. Leave a thin layer of joint compound beneath the tape.

3 Remove excess joint compound. Using the same drywall knife, make a final pass over the tape and bedding coat to remove any excess joint compound. Let this coat dry. Before applying the second (filler) coat, scrape or knock down any burrs or high spots. Take care not to cause gouges. If you do, apply a thin layer of joint compound to this area.

4 Apply the second coat, and remove excess. Load a hawk or mud tray with joint compound. Using a 10-inch straight-handled knife, apply a layer of joint compound as wide as the knife. Make it as smooth as you can, using repeat passes if necessary. Let the coat dry thoroughly. Again, use a scraper to knock down any burrs or high spots that you may have missed.

5 Apply the finish coat. Using a hawk or mud tray and a 10- or 12-inch finishing trowel, apply a wide finish coat to the taped joint. This should be a light skim coat. Move with long steady strokes, pulling in one direction and feathering out both edges to create the smoothest possible transition to the drywall face. Sand the joint if necessary.

1 Using a taping knife, apply a first coat of joint compound, about the width of the knife.

pro tip

IT'S EASY TO CHECK A DRYWALL JOINT FOR EXCESSIVE CROWNS OR RECESSES AFTER THE SECOND OR THIRD COAT OF JOINT COMPOUND. HOLD THE STRAIGHT EDGE OF A TROWEL ACROSS THE TOP OF THE JOINT, AND SEE WHETHER THERE IS A GAP BETWEEN THE JOINT COMPOUND AND THE ENDS OF THE TROWEL. IF THE GAP MEASURES MORE THAN $\frac{1}{16}$ INCH OR SO, YOU'LL NEED TO APPLY A WIDER SWATH OF JOINT COMPOUND AND FEATHER IT OUT MORE GRADUALLY.

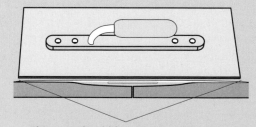

This gap should be no more than $\frac{1}{16}$".

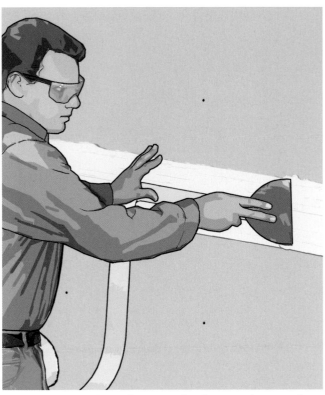

2 Embed the drywall tape in the first rough coat of joint compound, and smooth it against the wall with the taping knife.

3 Remove the excess mud from the edges around the tape with the same taping knife as before.

4 The 10-in.-wide filler coat can be applied with a straight-handled drywall knife or a finishing trowel.

5 For the finish coat, apply, smooth, and finish wet joint compound using a 12-in. finishing trowel.

TAPING FLUSH END-BUTT JOINTS

A FLUSH END-BUTT JOINT is more difficult to finish than a tapered joint because you have to put more work into feathering the layers of joint compound. Because there's no recess for it to sit in, the joint compound on finished end-butt joints will inevitably form a slight mound. The idea is to make this mound as inconspicuous as possible.

You'll need to feather out the edges of the joint to a greater width, leaving a wider seam than is required for factory tapered joints. A bump that is ⅛ inch high but 16 to 18 inches wide will seem flat to all but the closest inspections, but a narrower one can still be felt when you pass your hand over it.

Not only do end-butt joints require more work, they also provide slightly less stability than factory tapered joints, which makes them more likely to crack. To compensate for this, use fiberglass mesh tape (which adds strength) rather than paper tape.

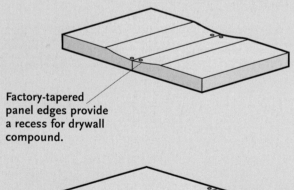

Factory-tapered panel edges provide a recess for drywall compound.

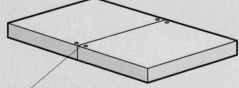

Flush end-butt joints must be carefully feathered to produce a smooth surface.

Drywall End and Edge Joints. Flush end-butt joints are formed wherever the untapered factory ends of drywall panels meet, where cut edges come together, or where an untapered end joins a factory tapered end. Unlike the joints formed by factory-tapered panel edges, end-butt joints provide no recess for joint compound.

Finishing Fastener Heads. Properly driven nails or screws, with shallow dimples, make finishing easier.

CLEANUP & MAINTAINANCE

JOINT COMPOUND cleans up easily using only water. By spraying the tools with a hose or a blast of water from a faucet, you can remove all joint compound, wet or dried. Use one knife to scrape another. **Note:** don't wash joint compound down the drain, as it can form sediment that may clog your pipes.

Once you've cleaned drywall knives, set them out to dry so that water runs off the blades and doesn't have a chance to pool on them. Otherwise, the blades will rust quickly. If they do rust or if you've missed some joint compound, simply sand them clean.

It's critical that you keep knife blades true and free of bends (except for the slight curves you may have introduced to help with crowning). To ensure this, store knives where they won't be bent or bowed beneath the weight of other tools.

Finishing Fastener Heads

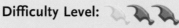

Difficulty Level:

TOOLS & MATERIALS
▮ Stepladder or scaffolding, as required
▮ 5- or 6-inch knife ▮ Joint compound
▮ 10- or 12-inch straight-handled knife
▮ 120-grit sandpaper or sanding sponge

1 Apply the first coat, and scrape flat. Using a 5- or 6-inch knife, apply a thin swath of joint compound over the fastener heads. This coat should merely fill in the dimple you created by driving or hammering the fastener. You can cover an entire row of them with one pass. This will make the joint compound less conspicuous. Let this first coat dry completely, and then scrape off any burrs or high spots that remain.

2 Apply a second coat, and scrape flat. Apply the second, slightly wider coat of joint compound to the fastener heads using a 10-inch straight-handled knife. Allow this coat to dry completely, and then scrape it smooth.

3 Apply the final coat. Using a 10-inch straight-handled knife, apply a third coat of joint compound that covers the second coat entirely. Carefully feather the edges, creating a gradual transition to the drywall surface. Allow this coat to dry completely, and sand it if necessary.

1 Rather than mudding nail- or screw-heads one at a time, you can cover them with long swaths of joint compound.

2 A larger swath of joint compound is easier to feather and blend into the face of the drywall panel.

3 The final coat of joint compound should be feathered out so thinly that it appears flat.

Taping an Inside Corner

Difficulty Level:

TOOLS & MATERIALS
- Stepladder or scaffolding, as required
- Paper drywall tape ▮ Tape bender
- 5- or 6-inch knife ▮ Joint compound
- Inside corner knife
- 10- or 12-inch straight-handled knife
- 120-grit sandpaper or sanding sponge

1 Prepare the drywall tape. Run a length of drywall tape along the inside corner, and cut the tape to size. Run the tape through your tape bender to fold it in half lengthwise. (Or fold it by hand.) Have this tape ready.

2 Apply the rough coat. Using a 5- or 6-inch knife, apply a 4-inch-wide layer of joint compound to both faces of the inside corner. Make this layer about ¼ inch thick.

3 Embed the tape and remove excess. While the first coat is still fresh and wet, use your fingers to embed the folded drywall tape into the compound. Use an inside corner knife or a regular 5-or 6-inch knife to seat the tape, drawing it firmly from ceiling to floor and squeezing out any excess joint compound from beneath the tape. Allow the first coat and tape to dry thoroughly before the next step. Scrape off any burrs or high spots.

4 Apply a second coat. Use a 10- or 12-inch straight-handled knife to apply a slightly wider layer of joint compound to each face of the inside corner. Be careful not to let the corner of the knife cut the tape. Feather the edges to the drywall faces. Let this coat of joint compound dry completely, and then scrape off any burrs or high spots.

5 Apply the finish coat. Using a 10- or 12-inch straight-handled knife, apply a top coat to each face of the inside corner. Feather the edges to create a gradual transition to the panel faces. At this point, you may want to use an inside corner knife to form a crisp, straight line where the two walls meet.

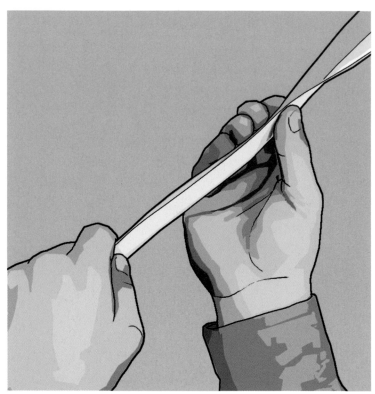

1 Paper drywall tape has a slight crease down its center, making it easy to fold in half for use in corners.

Taping an Inside Corner. Well-filled joints are particularly important at inside corners, which are susceptible to cracking.

2 Apply a rough coat, and embed a length of drywall tape (creased at its center line) the full length of the joint.

3 An inside corner knife enables you to embed the tape and smooth joint compound on both sides of a corner simultaneously.

4 Apply a filler coat over the embedded tape. Make this coat slightly wider than the first coat.

5 After the filler coat is dry, spread a finish coat on each face of the corner panels.

Taping & Finishing

Taping an Outside Corner

Difficulty Level:

TOOLS & MATERIALS
▌Stepladder or scaffolding, as required
▌5- or 6-inch knife ▌Joint compound
▌10- or 12-inch straight-handled knife
▌120-grit sandpaper or sanding sponge

NOTE: This procedure assumes that you've attached corner bead to the outside corner. If not, please refer to page 90 for instructions on installing it.

1 **Apply a first coat, and remove the excess.** Using a 5- or 6-inch taping knife, spread a 4-inch-wide layer of joint compound on each face of the outside corner. Corner bead has a raised edge, or bead, at the 90-degree bend that acts as a screed for your knife, helping you to create an evenly tapered layer of joint compound between the bead and panel face. As you smooth and feather the coat, keep the outermost point of this bead free of joint compound. Let this coat dry thoroughly, and then scrape off any burrs or high spots.

2 **Apply a second coat, and remove the excess.** Use a 10- or 12-inch straight-handled knife to apply a slightly wider layer of joint compound to both faces of the outside corner. Smooth and feather the coat to the drywall surface. Allow the coat to dry completely, and then scrape it smooth.

3 **Apply the finish coat.** Using a 10- or 12-inch straight-handled knife, apply a top coat to both faces of the corner. Feather the edges to make a gradual transition to the faces of the drywall panels, and sand the surfaces.

Corners. Outside corners, which are at risk to damage, are reinforced with metal or plastic bead before finishing.

1 Coat the corner bead with a layer of joint compound on each face of the outside corner's drywall panels.

2 No tape is used on an outside corner, but a second filler coat is applied. Corner bead has a raised edge at its corner, which supports the edge of the knife and leaves behind an even layer of joint compound.

3 Use a wide straight-handled knife to apply a final coat, feathering its edges as you blend it.

pro tip

A SMALL HOMEMADE DOLLY (ABOUT 20 TO 24 INCHES SQUARE) FITTED WITH 4-INCH CASTERS MAKES AN EXCELLENT HELPER FOR QUICKLY MOVING BUCKETS OF JOINT COMPOUND AROUND. IF YOU'RE WORKING OFF A STEPLADDER OR USING SHOE STILTS, YOU CAN STACK UP TWO OR THREE BUCKETS SO YOU DON'T HAVE TO BEND DOWN EVERY TIME YOU WANT TO RELOAD YOUR HAWK. CONSTRUCT THE DOLLY STRONG ENOUGH TO HANDLE ALL THAT WEIGHT—THREE BIG BUCKETS WEIGH 180 POUNDS WHEN FULL.

FINISH-SANDING

SANDING DRYWALL SEAMS involves two steps. Make a first pass using a sanding pole fitted with 120-grit sandpaper. Then hand-sand with 150-grit paper. For this step, fold the sandpaper in quarters, or attach it to a sanding block. (See page 116.)

As an alternative to this two-step process, you can sand with a fine screen mounted on a handle, or wet-sand (a dustless approach) using a small-celled polyurethane sponge designed for this purpose. Wet-sanding with one of these sponges does not yield as fine a finish as dry-sanding with 150-grit, but in situations that don't permit dust, it makes a good substitute for the pole-sanding/hand-sanding technique. If you're particularly sensitive to dust (or happen to have the equipment handy), you can use a commercial sanding machine with a wet/dry vacuum attachment for nearly dust-free sanding.

You'll find that lighting the work area carefully is essential to good finishing. If you shine light directly on a drywall joint, imperfections may not show up. Move the light to the side of the drywall, or shine it from above or below, and you're more likely to detect creases, recesses, bulges, and other defects. For this purpose, acquire a portable high-powered light source, such as a halogen lamp. Place it on a stand in order to free up both hands, or carry a portable light in one hand and sandpaper in the other as you return to survey the joints and spot-sand any imperfections.

If possible, seal off your work area to keep dust from drifting into finished rooms. To accomplish this,

Smooth Finish. Sanding is labor-intensive, and it produces a lot of fine, white dust, but painstaking sanding jobs make the smoothest walls.

set up a dust barrier of polyethylene sheets between the work space and all clean areas, and seal all four edges with masking tape. Keep in mind that joint-compound dust is very fine-grained and can escape through tiny cracks between doors and jambs or around unsealed dust barriers.

Taping & Finishing

Finish-Sanding

Difficulty Level:

TOOLS & MATERIALS
▌ Dust mask ▌ Hat
▌ Safety goggles
▌ Dust barriers (polyethylene)
▌ Portable, high-powered work light
▌ Pole sander with universal joint
▌ Sanding block
▌ Sanding screen
▌ 120- and 150-grit sandpaper
▌ Dry sanding sponge (if required)
▌ Wet/dry shop vacuum
▌ Broom and vacuum cleaner

1 Sand the joints smooth. Using a sanding pole loaded with 120-grit sandpaper, sand each of the joints if necessary. Keep edges smooth as you taper them into the face of the drywall. To avoid sanding through the top layers of joint compound and into the tape, apply gentle, even pressure, and resist the urge to bear down. If you do sand through to the tape, mark this area with a pencil, and reapply a coat of joint compound.

2 Check for imperfections. Before starting to finish-sand (with 150-grit paper), position your light so that it illuminates the seams you intend to sand. Lighting from the side will cast the light across imperfections and make them evident.

3 Finish-sand the joints. Using folded 150-grit paper, a sanding block loaded with 150-grit paper, a sanding screen, or a urethane sponge—depending on your preference and the job at hand—sand the seams and also the swaths of joint compound that cover fastener heads. Next, run your hand over the area to check for smoothness. On inside corners, where sanding blocks are hard to control, use just a folded sheet of paper for hand-sanding. Vacuum up drywall dust now, before you track it to other rooms and before you remove the dust barrier.

116

1 A sanding pole is an ideal tool for sanding drywall ceiling and wall seams.

2 Check the joints for smoothness with the palm of your hand, sanding down any high spots or bumps that you feel.

3 Hand-sanding may be required to get into corners. Using a sanding pole here may damage the seam.

SPECIAL FINISHES

Textured walls and ceilings add a low-tech, inexpensive design feature to any interior. These textures may appear difficult to achieve, but with a little practice, you can successfully imitate the effects of old-world craftsmen. Even better, they can hide some mistakes you may have made when hanging the panels. (And it's not even considered cheating!) Once you've practiced and experimented a bit on scrap drywall, you'll have the skills to texture your own walls or ceilings using basic tools and materials.

No matter what type of texture you intend to apply, you must first complete all joints and fastener heads as described earlier in this book. Although texturing can hide errors, it provides no substitute for proper finish work. Before you texture, finish and prepare all drywall panels just as you would for painting (although there is no need to be as fussy as you would be for a painted wall).

All But the Final Finish. This room, having been taped, finish-coated, and sanded, is ready for painting or texture finishing.

Applying an Orange-Peel Texture

Difficulty Level:

TOOLS & MATERIALS
▌ Stepladder or scaffolding, as required
▌ Water
▌ Bucket of joint compound, half full
▌ Mixer or mixing stick
▌ ½-inch-nap roller
▌ Roller pan
▌ Test scrap of drywall, approximately 2 x 2 feet
▌ 18- to 24-inch straightedge or finishing knife

You can apply a textured finish using an airless paint sprayers (see page 123), but there are a number of hand-applied textures that will give you a professional-looking finish. For example, to achieve an orange-peel finish without a sprayer, simply use a paint roller to apply watered-down joint compound.

If the roller produces the texture you want, allow it to dry as is. However, you may have trouble getting a good orange-peel effect using this approach, especially on inside corners (though this can be achieved with practice and patience). If this is the case, try knocking down the half-dry surface. This usually improves the appearance of this texture, making it more consistent with an orange-peel look.

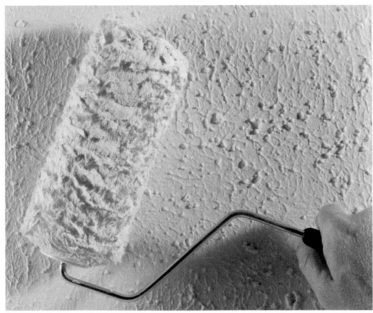

Orange Peel. This texture can be applied using a paint roller (shown before being flattened with the knockdown technique).

1 Thin joint compound. Choose a bucket of joint compound that is at least half full, but not one that is brand-new and filled to the top. Add some water to the bucket of joint compound—you'll need enough to make it spreadable with a roller but not runny. (See next step.)

2 Mix the thinned compound. Using a hand mixer or a mixing paddle chucked into an electric drill, or by hand, mix the water and joint compound until its consistency matches that of paint or very heavy cream. (If it doesn't seem thin enough, add more water and mix again. If you think you added too much water, add some more undiluted joint compound. Experiment with small batches to derive the right proportion of water to add.)

3 Check the mixture's consistency. Pour some of the mixture into a roller pan. Using a roller, apply it to a piece of scrap drywall held upright. The mixture should not sag or run. If it runs, add more joint compound; if it turns out to be too thick to roll, add more water.

4 Roll a first coat onto the wall. Using the ½-inch-nap roller, apply the mixture to the wall. Roll it as you would roll on paint, covering every square inch of the wall. Get as close to the corners and edges as possible. Allow this application to dry for 10 minutes or until it loses its shine.

5 Roll on a second coat. After the first coat has dried, roll on a second coat. Work the roller over the surface until you achieve the desired effect. Make sure that you're satisfied with it because you shouldn't touch the wall again except to paint it. Wash out the roller with water. Cap the joint-compound bucket, and then date it and label it "orange peel" so you won't mistake it for standard joint compound on future projects.

Knocking down the finish. As an alternative, you can modify orange-peel texture to give it a knocked-down look. Holding an 18- to 24-inch rigid straightedge or finishing knife almost flat to the wall, draw it across the half-dry orange peel finish, applying extremely light pressure. Check your work as you go because the finish you leave will be the final look. You can vary the finish by applying more or less pressure.

1 The joint compound needs to be diluted until it can be rolled on the wall with a paint roller.

2 The easiest way to mix joint compound is to use a mixing paddle and a power drill.

3 Before applying the texture, test the joint compound's consistency on a piece of scrap drywall.

4 For a straight orange-peel finish, first apply watered-down joint compound with a ½-in.-nap roller.

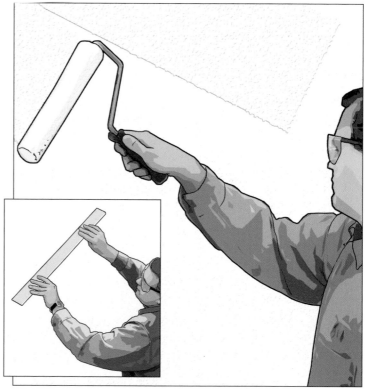

5 After the first coat has dried for at least 10 minutes, roll on a second coat. To knock down the texture, draw an 18- to 24-in. straightedge lightly across the wet surface.

Applying a Brocade Finish

Difficulty Level:

TOOLS & MATERIALS
▌ Stepladder or scaffolding, as required
▌ 10- or 12-inch drywall knife
▌ Mud pan or hawk ▌ Joint compound
▌ 5- or 6-inch knife

You can create this unusual finish using unthinned joint compound and a flat metal or wooden hand trowel. The finish looks as if someone spread joint compound onto the surface and then flattened it while it was still wet, without swiping across it to smooth it out. This is exactly what you'll do to apply this finish, working in 4-foot-square sections at a time. This treatment is typically used on ceilings.

1 **Spread joint compound onto the wall.** Using a 10- or 12-inch knife, apply a thin coat of joint compound to a 4 × 4-foot area of the ceiling (or wall). Do not try to smooth the joint compound out, but leave it in an irregular pattern with relatively uniform thickness.

2 **Flatten it with a trowel.** Using a drywall knife or hand trowel, flatten the peaks of the wet joint compound by pressing the trowel against the surface and pulling it squarely away. Do not swipe laterally to smooth out the finish. Work the wet joint compound to your liking at this time; the texture you leave behind with the trowel will remain as the final finish.

1 Spread a thin layer of joint compound on a small section of wall using a 10- or 12-in. drywall knife.

2 Using a small drywall knife, flatten the surface out in small areas, leaving behind a textured pattern.

Getting the Look of Fabric. A brocade finish imitates the look of brocade, a fabric with a raised design.

Applying a Stucco Finish

Difficulty Level:

TOOLS & MATERIALS
- Stepladder or scaffolding, as required
- Mud pan or hawk ▮ Joint compound
- 10- or 12-inch knife (for application)
- 5-inch knife, notched trowel, graining comb

A Spanish-style finish, one that resembles fancy stucco, is simple to achieve and does an excellent job of concealing any imperfections. You just apply an ⅛-inch-thick layer of joint compound and then make random curved swaths in the wet material with a 5-inch drywall knife. If you'd prefer a broader pattern, use a notched trowel instead; for a narrower pattern, use a paint graining comb or even a regular plastic hair comb. Because this relatively thick layer takes more time to dry, you can work a larger area than those on which you use thinned-out compound.

1 Spread joint compound onto the wall. Using a 10- or 12-inch drywall knife, apply a thin layer of joint compound to the ceiling or wall.

2 Make stucco patterns in the wet joint compound. While the joint compound is still wet, use a 5-inch drywall knife (or notched trowel, paint graining comb, or other tool) to make circular or swath patterns as desired. Overlap the textured areas slightly so that the entire surface is covered.

1 Because you can work quickly when creating a stucco-style finish, you can apply joint compound to a larger area.

2 To achieve stucco-style texturing, use a notched trowel to make curved patterns in the wet joint compound.

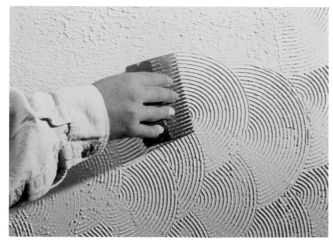

Spanish Style. A stucco finish can be made using various tools, such as the paint-graining comb shown here.

APPLYING BRUSH AND ROLLER TEXTURES

ALMOST ANY IMPLEMENT will leave some type of pattern in wet joint compound. Jab-and-dab techniques make use of textured brushes to create distinctive patterns, and you can achieve similar effects using textured rollers. For either of these methods, apply thinned joint compound to the wall or ceiling surface as described for the orange-peel surfaces. (See page 118.) Then, while the mixture is wet, you can jab and dab at it with a sponge like the one shown (or a special brush), or you can roll it using a textured roller.

Textured roller sleeves resemble those used for conventional paint rolling, except that they're covered with a pattern of plastic strands or wires. When rolled across wet joint compound, these strands or wires leave behind a random pattern.

Another textured look can be achieved using a textured brush. This tool resembles a two-headed, side-by-side cloth mop. A handle yokes the two heads, making it easy to press the device into the wet joint compound as you move randomly across the surface to create the texturing. Apply it to the same thinned joint compound that you'd use for the orange-peel textured finish. With a smaller brush or even a sponge, you can make smaller patterns, but this will be a lot more labor-intensive and tedious.

Jab-and-Dab Techniques. You can buy custom-made brushes, but even a sponge will work in wet mud.

Textured Roller Covers. Made for painting, a texture roller can be easily used for applying joint compound.

pro tip

A COUPLE OF GALLONS OF WET JOINT COMPOUND IS HEAVY AND CUMBERSOME, AS ANYONE WHO'S HOISTED A BUCKET OF IT KNOWS. IF YOUR CEILING JOISTS ARE SPACED MORE THAN 16 INCHES ON CENTER OR IF YOU'VE USED THINNER PANELS, THERE'S A GOOD CHANCE THAT THE CEILING WILL START TO SAG UNDER THE WEIGHT OF A TEXTURED FINISH, WHICH IS HEAVIER THAN A PAINTED FINISH. IF THESE CONDITIONS EXIST BUT YOUR HEART IS SET ON A TEXTURED CEILING, FINISH IT WITH A LIGHTER, VERMICULITE- OR POLYSTYRENE-BASED BLOWN TEXTURE. (SEE "APPLYING SPRAYED FINISHES," OPPOSITE.)

APPLYING SPRAYED FINISHES

UNLIKE MOST TEXTURING TREATMENTS, blown ceilings and walls require advanced skill and equipment that most people will have to rent. A popcorn-like material (polystyrene or vermiculite) is fed from a hopper to an airless spray gun, which is attached to an air compressor. Once it is blown onto the surface, it is left to dry without retouching. This texturing takes some practice to apply properly, so consider hiring a painting or drywall contractor to do the work for you if you have no experience with it.

Another common treatment is an orange-peel finish. You create this texture by spraying watered-down joint compound through an airless paint sprayer. If left to dry untouched, the surface will resemble that of an orange peel. However, you must add just the right proportion of water, and mastering the spraying technique takes lots of practice. (An orange-peel finish can also be applied by hand.)

Sprayed Finishes. Fed through a hopper into a spray gun, popcorn-like material is blown to create a textured surface and left to dry without retouching.

GREEN OR NATURAL PAINTS

IF YOU OPT FOR A PAINTED FINISH, consider a "greener" paint. Paints produce VOCs (volatile organic compounds) that are harmful. Combine that with tight-home construction where outdoor fresh air is limited due to energy concerns, and the typical weekend painting project can lead to health problems. There are three general types of green paint: natural paints, zero-VOC paints, and low-VOC paints.

Natural Paints. Natural paints are water-based products made from such ingredients as water, essential oils, clay, and even milk and milk-byproducts. Linseed oil and citrus oil are also used in some of the natural wood stains, oils, and waxes used for natural finishes on wood. These natural paint products could also be categorized as zero-VOC products because they do not off gas, unless you consider the smell of essential oils and citrus a product of off gassing. Search "natural paints" on the Internet.

Zero-VOC paints. The Environmental Protection Agency has set VOC limits for paint. To be considered a zero-VOC paint, it must contain less than 5 grams per liter.

Low-VOC Paints. Low-VOC paints and finishes are almost invariably water-based, although some alkyd paints qualify. To meet the EPA standard that allows the use of the "low-VOC" label on the can, they must contain less than 250 grams per liter for latex paint and 380 for alkyd paint.

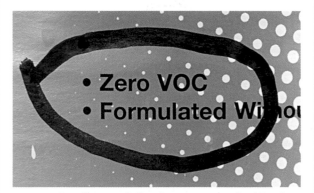

"Green" Paint. Look for the zero-VOC designation on the paint label. Paints must meet standards of the EPA and are certified by independent groups.

Skim-Coating

Difficulty Level: 🐟🐟🐟

TOOLS & MATERIALS
▪ Joint compound ▪ Water ▪ Mixer ▪ Roller pan
▪ ⅜-inch-nap roller ▪ 18- to 24-inch finishing knife

Occasionally, you'll encounter a drywalling phenomenon known as ghosting or photographing. These terms refer to when the seams and patches of joint compound show through the layers of paint. This can happen because the joint compound and drywall face paper have different porosities and therefore absorb paint differently. The problem tends to show up most noticeably with gloss paints and in rooms with a lot of natural light.

There are two ways to reduce photographing. You can paint the drywall with a primer-sealer. These high-tech products have a high resin content that help hide the seams. If you'd prefer a more traditional method, you can skim-coat the entire wall with a thin layer of joint compound. This will ensure that every square inch has about the same porosity. Skim-coating also helps make new drywall blend in better with old plaster. Here's how to apply a skim coat using a conventional nap roller.

Pre-Priming. You can apply a coating of watery joint compound to walls to provide a consistent surface for priming.

1 Prepare the wall and the joint compound. Tape, finish, and sand the drywall joints as explained on pages 107–116. (Skim-coating does not take the place of proper finish work.) Thin the joint compound with water to the consistency of paint or heavy cream.

2 Blend the joint compound. Mix the watered-down joint compound by hand or by using a mixing paddle chucked into an electric drill. Then pour or scoop out this mixture into a roller pan.

3 Apply the skim coat. Roll a thin layer of the new mix onto the wall, just as you would a coat of paint or primer. This thinned mixture will dry quickly, so work just one wall at a time. (A roller cover with a thick nap will give the surface a slight texture; if you want perfectly smooth walls, use the lowest-nap roller cover available, and apply an even thinner mixture.)

4 Smooth out the wet skim coat. As soon as you've rolled out the thinned joint compound, quickly smooth it with broad, continuous strokes of an 18- to 24-inch finishing knife (or the widest knife or trowel that you have available). Work from the top of the wall to the bottom. You can sand out small ridges later, but try to get the skim coat as smooth and consistent as possible using quick troweling strokes of the knife.

1 For skim-coating, joint compound needs to be watered down to the texture of paint.

2 Thinned joint compound should be mixed thoroughly, either by hand or with power-driven mixing paddles.

3 To defeat photographing (where joint compound absorbs paint differently from drywall), skim-coat the wall by rolling on a thin layer of thinned joint compound.

4 Before the rolled-on drywall compound dries, smooth it with a wide straight-handled finishing knife.

7 repairing drywall

NO MATTER HOW GOOD A DRYWALL JOB YOU DO, lots of unavoidable things can happen to create flaws. A new house can settle during its first couple of years, causing cracks to develop in corners or along ceiling joints. In both new and old houses, the moisture level changes seasonally, shrinking window and door frames, pulling the framing away from the drywall panels, and even causing drywall nailheads to pop.

STRUCTURAL CHANGES in the house don't get all the credit for drywall damage. A slip of the wrist as you're moving a table can leave a nasty gash. An errant basketball thrown indoors can make a conspicuous dent. How do you fix problems like these? Well, some you can take care of with a little joint compound, a strip of tape, and a sanding sponge. Others may require wood backing or screening.

REPAIR BASICS

Bulging or Recessed Drywall

Recessed or bulging drywall can usually be traced to the framing. A misaligned stud stands either *shy* or *proud* of the partition line. In other words, it recedes from or protrudes beyond the plane formed by the row of stud edges that make up a wall.

If the stud is causing a bulge, there's not much you can do to correct it once the drywall has been hung. This problem should have been fixed beforehand by correcting the stud or by removing and replacing it with one that aligns properly with the partition line. (See "Correcting Framing Mistakes," page 46.) To hide the bulge at this point, you need to fill in the void on the sides of bulge by apply an extra-wide (20-inch) layer of joint compound, and feather it out carefully.

If the stud stands shy of the partition line, causing a recess, the problem is relatively easy to fix, provided the stud does not support either end of the drywall panel and the panel is not fastened with adhesive. Before you apply any joint compound, remove the fasteners, or simply drive them all the way through the panel and into the stud so that they no longer hold the drywall against it. Don't drive any additional fasteners; instead, apply joint compound to conceal the old fastener holes.

If the stud coincides with a panel end, then it must have fasteners to support the panel. In this case (or if the panel is fastened with adhesive), build up the recessed joint with multiple and ever-wider layers of joint compound until it comes flush with the rest of the wall.

FIXING BULGING OR RECESSED DRYWALL

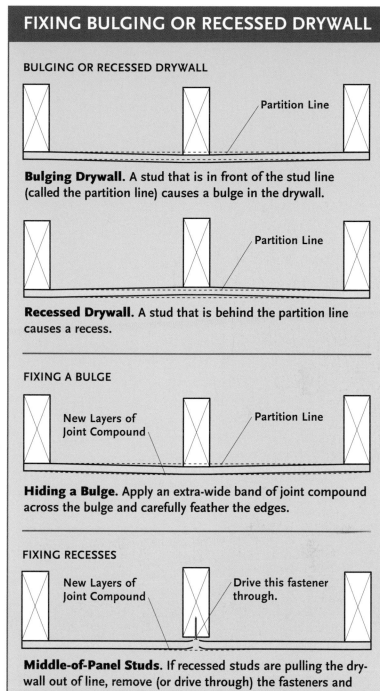

BULGING OR RECESSED DRYWALL

Partition Line

Bulging Drywall. A stud that is in front of the stud line (called the partition line) causes a bulge in the drywall.

Partition Line

Recessed Drywall. A stud that is behind the partition line causes a recess.

FIXING A BULGE

New Layers of Joint Compound   Partition Line

Hiding a Bulge. Apply an extra-wide band of joint compound across the bulge and carefully feather the edges.

FIXING RECESSES

New Layers of Joint Compound   Drive this fastener through.

Middle-of-Panel Studs. If recessed studs are pulling the drywall out of line, remove (or drive through) the fasteners and apply joint compound over the old fastener holes.

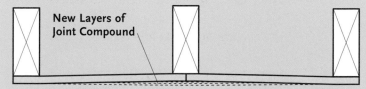

New Layers of Joint Compound

End-of-Panel Studs. If the panel must have fasteners (if it is a stud at either end of the drywall panel), build up the recess with repeated and ever-wider layers of joint compound until the recess comes flush with the faces of the drywall panels.

FIXING POPPED NAILS OR SCREWS

NAIL POP refers to nails or screws that show their heads after the drywall job has been taped, finished, and painted. If nail pop occurs near the end of a drywalling job but before you paint, just the pressure of a paint roller can force a nail- or screwhead through the finished surface. Typically, however, nails won't pop until months later.

Nail pop can occur wherever there is space between the back side of the panel and the face of the framing member to which it is attached. One of two events usually accounts for such a space: either the drywaller neglected to hold the panel firmly against the stud face while fastening it, or the stud contained excessive moisture when it was installed, and as it dried, it warped or shrank away from the drywall, leaving a gap. In either case, a slight pressure applied to the drywall face is all it takes. Sometimes, in fact, nail pop doesn't require even that: nail- or screwheads can reveal themselves with the normal shrinkage of framing lumber as the house dries out over its first year, especially during the first winter, when it is heated.

If you have the opportunity, take preventive measures. Frame with stable lumber that has been dried to the proper moisture content. When hanging panels, apply mastic adhesive to the studs, and then drive in two nails at each location, spacing them about 2 inches apart. Make sure that you hold the drywall securely against the stud before driving nails or screws.

To fix a panel with popped nails or screws, first remove the protruding fasteners—or, easier still, drive them in farther until their heads sit just below the surface of the face paper. Next, drive screws or nails 1½ inches above and below (or to each side of) the popped fastener. This will secure the drywall against the framing. Lastly, treat the area with three coats of joint compound, scraping each dry coat before applying the next. You'll notice that some nail pops will disappear on their own as the house expands and contracts from season to season.

Nail Popping. This can occur when framing members shrink behind drywall panels. Drive the protruding fasteners through, and then add additional fasteners 1½ in. on each side to bring the drywall back against the framing.

FIXING BROKEN OR BLOWN-OUT DRYWALL

IF YOU MISCUT A PANEL that has to fit around a utility box or into an inside corner and then force it into place instead of trimming it, the panel will likely blow out, tearing the face paper and cracking the gypsum within. This can also happen where a door or window frame has been misaligned with the partition line or at a corner that is significantly out of plumb.

To repair a blown-out section of drywall, cut away all the torn paper using a utility knife, and clean out the loose gypsum. Next, use a 5- or 6-inch knife to apply a coat of joint compound. Smooth this coat flush with the face of the panel; allow it to dry thoroughly; and then follow the usual three-layer taping procedure described in Chapter 6, page 108.

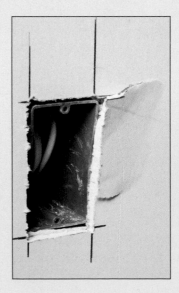

Fixing Blowouts. If a drywall panel hasn't been cut exactly to size around utility boxes and inside corners or if door and window frames are out of the partition line, the panel that is forced into place will likely blow out. Fix blowouts by cutting away loose drywall with a utility knife and applying new layers of joint compound.

FIXING BAD END-BUTT JOINTS

FLUSH END-BUTT JOINTS occur where the un-tapered ends or handmade cuts on drywall panels meet one another. Because the ends don't have the slight taper provided along the factory edges to accommodate the joint compound, these joints tend to bulge once they've been taped and finished. Once you've created these crowns, it's difficult to knock them down without damaging the finish. To make an end-butt joint crown less conspicuous, apply a 20-inch-wide seam of joint compound, and feather the edges down gradually to the drywall face.

CLEANING UP DRIED COMPOUND

ON A TYPICAL JOB, joint compound tends to end up all over the place. Gobs of this wet, sloppy substance fall to the floor or get splattered onto nearby walls. You'll find that "mud" cleans up much more easily when it's still wet. Simply scoop it up with a 5-inch drywall knife, and then follow with a damp rag or sponge to wipe up the remaining smear. If the joint compound has been left to dry, chip away at the hardened mound with the same tool. In most cases, it will break free. Again, follow with a wet cloth or sponge to get the last of it up.

PATCHING PLASTER

REPAIRING PLASTER DAMAGE is usually more involved than fixing drywall problems. Small cracks and gouges in plaster can all be repaired with a thin coat of drywall joint compound. But deeper and wider cracks require a different approach. The damaged area first has to be cleaned so it's free of dust and plaster debris. Then the hole must be filled to just below the surrounding surface with patching plaster. Once dry, the repair can be completed with a smooth coat of joint compound.

Difficulty Level:

TOOLS & MATERIALS
- Patching plaster or joint compound
- Spray bottle filled with clean water
- Paint roller and roller tray
- 6- and 10-in. taping knife

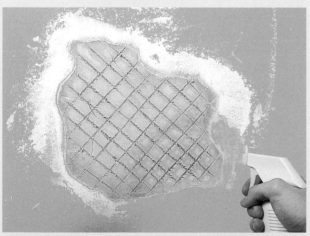

1 Use patching plaster to fill most of the repair hole. Mix it according to the package directions, and spread it using a 6-in. taping knife. Once the plaster is almost dry, mark a crosshatch pattern in the surface to create better bonding for the joint compound. Before applying the joint compound, spray the surface with water.

2 Cover the patching plaster with a coat of drywall joint compound. Use a 10- or 12-in.-wide taping knife to get the smoothest surface. Rest one corner of the blade on the wall, and pull the knife over the patch. Once the joint compound is dry, sand it flush to the surrounding surface using 100-grit sandpaper. Remove the sanding dust, prime, and paint.

Repairing Drywall

FIXES AND REPAIRS

Making Repairs before Painting

Difficulty Level: 🔧🔧🔧

TOOLS & MATERIALS
- Putty knife ▪ Utility knife ▪ Dust mask
- Palm sander ▪ Joint compound ▪ Safety goggles
- 10-in. drywall knife ▪ Paint ▪ Paintbrush
- Stepladder (if needed)

1 **Scrap away damaged areas.** Use a putty knife to scrape off any loose or flaking paint until you have a solid, smooth wall surface. Avoid digging the knife blade deeply into the gypsum core of the drywall. If the outside paper is torn, cut it using a sharp utility knife so the remaining paper has a solid edge.

2 **Sand and patch the area.** Lightly sand any damaged areas to smooth the edges; then cover the damage with joint compound. Use a 10-in. knife to get the widest and smoothest patch.

3 **Finish sand the area and prime the patch.** After the compound is dry, sand it smooth using a sanding block or an orbital sander with 120-grit sandpaper. Wipe away any dust; then prime each spot using primer paint.

1 Remove paint if any is present (inset). Even on new jobs, drywall paper can tear. Use a sharp utility knife to remove loose paper.

2 Sand the edges of the torn area using sandpaper around a sanding block or a palm sander. Apply a layer of joint compound using a wide knife.

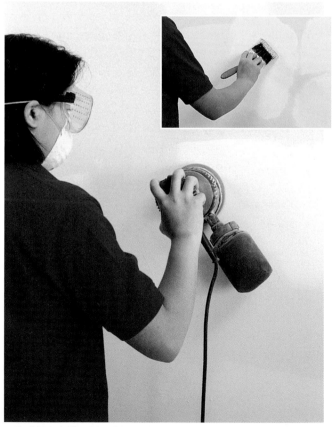

3 When dry, sand the patched area smooth using a palm sander. Be sure to wear a mask. When satisfied, clean the area, and then prime the patches (inset).

130

Fixing Cracks and Gashes

Difficulty Level:

TOOLS & MATERIALS
❚ Utility knife
❚ Mesh or paper tape
❚ Joint compound
❚ 6- and 10-inch taping knives
❚ 120-grit sandpaper

You can repair stress cracks or minor gashes in drywall easily, using only joint compound and mesh tape. With most cracks, there is no need to cut out and patch sections of drywall; you don't have to provide backing if the cut does not go all the way through the panel. Simply treat it as though it were a drywall joint that you were finishing from scratch. Apply tape over the damaged area, and apply the customary three coats, sanding the final coat as necessary.

1 **Prepare the crack.** Clean out the crack by making a V-shaped cut along its length with a utility knife or small putty knife. Undercut slightly to create a key for the patching material to grab on to. Carve out all of the loose or broken gypsum, and clean off any torn face paper. Push on the panel around the crack. If the panel shows any movement, drive fasteners along each side of the crack into the nearest framing members. This will help to stabilize the panel and prevent further movement.

2 **Apply the first coat of joint compound.** If you're using mesh tape, apply it directly to the crack, and then spread a first coat (the rough coat) of joint compound over the tape. (If you're using paper tape, apply the rough coat first and embed the tape in it. Fiberglass mesh tape is recommended for fixing cracks, because the seams don't require strength as much as they do flexibility.) Smooth out the joint compound, feathering its edges. Let this coat dry completely.

3 **Apply subsequent coats, and then sand smooth.** Using a taping knife as a scraper, knock down any burrs or high spots on the first coat. Then apply a second coat of joint compound, and let it dry thoroughly. Scrape down any burrs or high spots on this coat. Apply a third coat of joint compound; allow it to dry; and then sand this final coat with sandpaper or a sanding sponge to a finished smoothness.

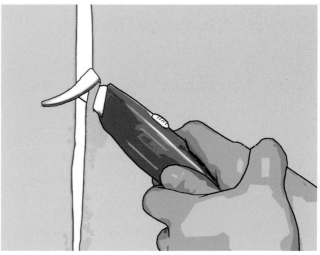

1 Use a utility knife to clean out a crack before applying any joint compound.

2 If you are using mesh tape, apply it directly over the crack before applying joint compound. Note that fasteners have been driven to either side of the crack.

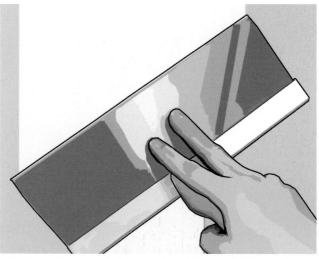

3 As with seam finishing, the wider and thinner the final coat is layed on, the less obvious it will be.

Repairing Drywall

Patching a Small Hole

Difficulty Level:

TOOLS & MATERIALS
- Mesh or paper tape ▪ Utility knife
- 6-and 10-inch taping knives
- Joint compound ▪ 120-grit sandpaper

1 Clean the hole, and then apply the rough coat and tape. Clean the drywall around the hole, cutting away all the loose or broken gypsum and trimming back any torn face paper. Apply two or three pieces of mesh drywall tape across the hole in an X pattern, or spread a coat of joint compound and embed paper tape.

2 Apply a second coat. Apply joint compound on top of the tape, smooth it out, and then carefully blend the edges into the wall. Let this coat dry completely.

3 Apply two finish coats. Using a 6-inch taping knife as a scraper, knock down any burrs or high spots. Apply another coat of joint compound; smooth it out; and feather the edges down to the wall surface. After this coat has dried, knock down any burrs or high spots. Then apply a final coat of joint compound; allow it to dry; and sand it to a finished smoothness.

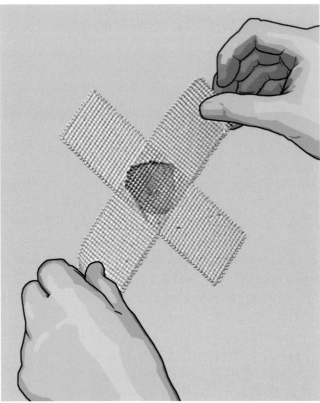

1 For extra strength over a small hole, make an X with two pieces of fiberglass mesh or paper drywall tape.

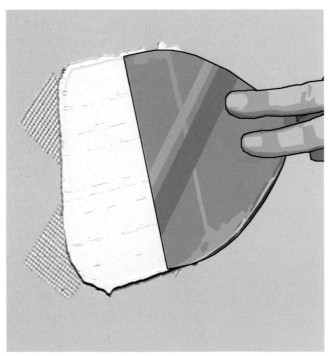

2 Apply and smooth out the first coat of joint compound with a 6-in. taping knife.

3 Apply the finish coat of joint compound using a wider knife, and feather it out as thinly as possible.

Fixing Cracks in Corners

Difficulty Level:

TOOLS & MATERIALS
▮ Utility knife
▮ Joint compound (and paper tape if necessary)
▮ 5- or 6-inch taping knife
▮ 10- or 12-inch taping knife
▮ 120-grit sandpaper

When drywall cracks in an inside corner, it usually means that the supporting framing has shifted or the foundation has settled. A new house often takes a year or more to settle out entirely, but older houses are still settling as well, causing cracks to appear—most often in corners. You can solve this problem one of two ways, depending on the size of the crack. If it's just a hairline, simply apply a bead of white latex silicon caulk. If the crack is larger, you'll need to apply joint compound with a large drywall knife (or inside corner knife) and smooth it to a sandable finish.

1 Prepare the crack, and apply a first coat. Using a utility knife, clean out the crack, removing any loose joint compound. Then, with a 5- or 6-inch taping knife, apply a layer of joint compound, carefully working it into the crack. (In some cases, especially for large cracks, you may want to use tape as well.) Let this coat dry completely before moving on to the next step.

2 Apply the finish coats. After knocking down any burrs or high spots with a taping knife, apply a second layer of compound using a larger knife. Smooth it out, carefully feathering the edges to the drywall surface. Let this coat dry. Two coats may fill the crack adequately, but you might want to apply (and sand) a third coat if the patch still needs to be feathered into the face of the drywall.

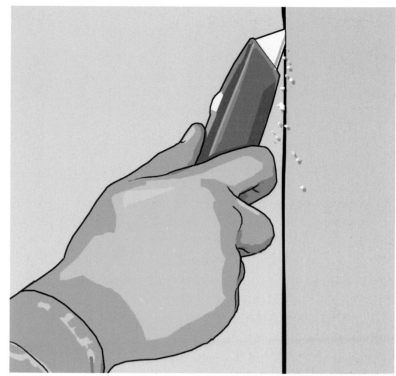

1 Cracks in corners may occur as framing shifts and dries, or when a structure settles. First clean out the area using a utility knife or small putty knife, and then apply a coat of joint compound with a 5- or 6-in. taping knife.

2 Use a wide taping knife to apply the second coat, feathering the compound into the wall surface. A third coat may be needed.

Repairing Drywall

Fixing a Larger Hole

Difficulty Level:

TOOLS & MATERIALS
❙ Utility knife or saw
❙ Furring strips or wood blocks, drill, and screws
❙ Patching drywall
❙ Mesh or paper tape
❙ Joint compound and taping knives
❙ 120-grit sandpaper

1 **Prepare the hole and add backing.** Create a patch by cutting a squared-off section of drywall larger than the damaged area. Trace the outlines of the patch onto the wall. Use the outline to cut a square or rectangular opening in the wall. Cut furring strips or wood blocks that bridge the hole. You'll insert them behind the drywall panel to provide a screwing base for the patch.

2 **Fasten the backing to the wall.** Drive drywall screws through the panel around the perimeter of the hole to secure the furring strips or blocks. Use at least two screws per piece of wood.

3 **Attach the patch to the backing.** Trim the patch to make it slightly smaller than the hole you've cut into the wall; you can fill any small gaps with joint compound. Screw through the drywall patch and into the blocks or furring to hold it securely in place. Depending on the size of the patch, add a screw every 5 or 6 inches or enough to make sure the patch is held securely in place.

4 **Apply joint compound and tape.** Spread a coat of joint compound to fill the gap between the patch and the surrounding drywall. Embed tape in this wet first coat, and apply a layer of joint compound over the tape, just as you would if you were taping a seam between two drywall panels. Smooth out the coat, and let it dry thoroughly.

5 **Apply two finish coats.** Apply a second layer of joint compound on top of the drywall tape. Smooth it out, and carefully blend the edges into the wall. Let this coat dry completely. Knock down any burrs or high spots with a taping knife. Apply a third coat; allow it to dry; and sand it to a finished smoothness. Remember to feather the compound well beyond the original damage to help the patch blend with the surrounding wall. Prime the patch before painting.

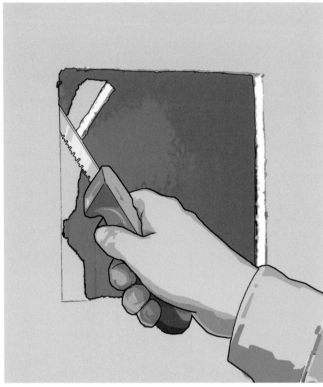

1 A rectangular hole with straight, evenly cut sides will be easier to patch than a ragged one.

Large Holes. The bigger the hole, the more backing it will need to minimize stress on the finished joints and prevent the patch from falling back into the wall cavity.

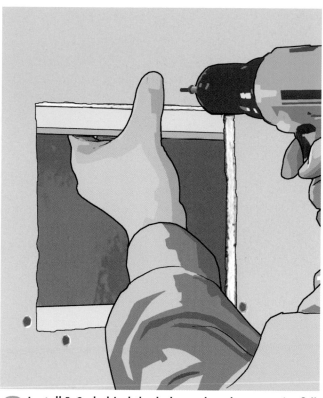

2 Install 1x3s behind the hole so that they span its full width, with an overlap of 1½ in. to either side.

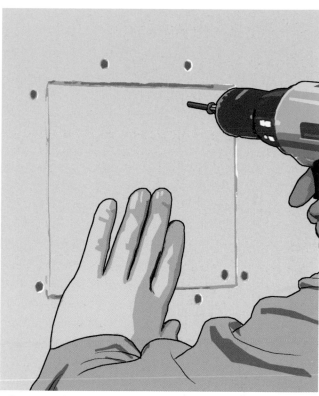

3 Cut a drywall patch, and screw it in place by driving screws into the furring strips beneath.

4 Apply a coat of joint compound to fill the gaps between the patch and the drywall panel, and then embed the drywall tape.

5 Apply the second coat after the first has dried. A thin final coat will make the patch appear seamless after it's sanded.

Repairing Drywall

Patching over a Removed Utility Box

Difficulty Level:

TOOLS & MATERIALS
■ Measuring tape ■ Patching drywall
■ Utility knife or saw and surface-forming tool
■ Joint compound and taping knives
■ Drywall tape ■ 120-grit sandpaper

When you permanently remove a utility or switch box, there remains a small rectangular hole in the drywall. A patch this small doesn't need backing, because the joint compound will hold it in place. To keep this small, unbacked patch from falling through the hole, bevel the edges of both hole and patch to form complementary angles.

1 Prepare the hole. Bevel the edges of the drywall around the perimeter of the hole so that they flare outward from the hole about ½ inch—the perimeter of the hole on the wall surface will now be somewhat larger than the perimeter of the hole in the back. Make the bevel approximately 45 degrees, but don't bother checking the angle for accuracy.

2 Cut a patch to fit. Measure the beveled hole, and then cut a piece of drywall that will cover it to the outside edges. Then bevel the patch piece on all four sides, matching the bevel angle to that of the hole. A surface-forming tool or a sanding block will help to quickly smooth and true up the beveled edges. Test-fit the patch, and trim it as needed.

3 Cover the edges of the patch with joint compound. Before inserting the patch, butter it by applying a sufficient layer of joint compound to all four of its beveled edges.

4 Install the patch. Firmly push the patch into place so that the joint compound oozes out of the seams. Using a 5- or 6-inch drywall knife, smooth the squeezed-out joint compound, and add more if necessary to make enough for a bedding coat. Embed drywall tape in this wet coat; cover it with more joint compound; and carefully feather this layer down to the face of the drywall. Let this coat dry completely before moving on.

5 Finish the seams. First, knock down any burrs or high spots that appear on the previous coat. Then apply a second layer of joint compound. Smooth it out, blending the edges into the wall. Let this coat dry thoroughly. Scrape down this second coat, and then apply a third coat, covering the patch. Let it dry, and sand it to a finished smoothness.

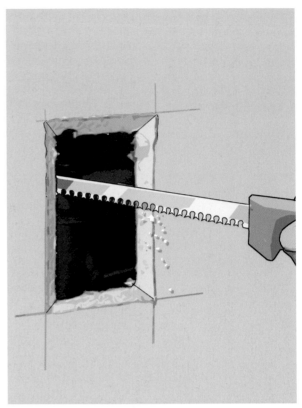

1 For a small patch with no backing, like the one shown here, first bevel the perimeter of the hole.

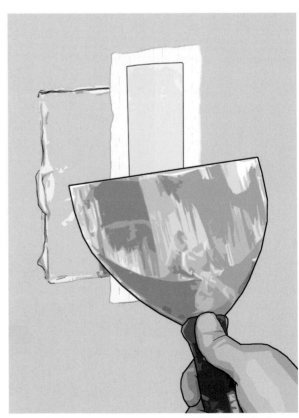

4 After pushing the patch into the flared hole, coat and tape the entire patch and its seams.

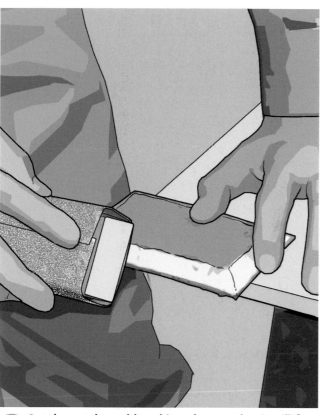

2 Cut the patch, and bevel its edges so that it will fit neatly, like a plug, into the hole.

3 Butter the edges of the patch with a substantial layer of joint compound.

5 The utility-box patch should be finished with a final, thin coat of joint compound, and sanded smooth.

pro tip

WHEN WORKING WITH WIRING, YOU'LL NEED TO EXERCISE SOME BASIC PRECAUTIONS. IF YOU'RE REMOVING A RECEPTACLE, FIRST REMOVE THE FUSE OR FLIP THE CIRCUIT BREAKER FOR THE BOX BEFORE YOU TOUCH IT—AND CHECK THE BOX AGAIN WITH A VOLTAGE TESTER BEFORE YOU GO AT IT WITH A SCREWDRIVER. NEVER BURY A BROKEN OR UNUSED BOX BENEATH THE WALL—ALWAYS REMOUNT THE BOX IN A NEW LOCATION BEFORE PATCHING THE HOLE. DON'T TOUCH WIRES BEHIND THE WALL, EVEN IF IT'S JUST TO MOVE THEM OUT OF THE WAY, WITHOUT FIRST TESTING THEM WITH A VOLTAGE TESTER.

Repairing Drywall

Patching over a Removed Window or Door

Difficulty Level:

TOOLS & MATERIALS
▌Standard carpenter's hand tools
▌10d nails ▌2x4 or 2x6 lumber
▌Utility knife ▌Drywall
▌1⅛-inch Type W drywall screws and screw gun
▌Mesh or paper drywall tape
▌Joint compound ▌6-inch taping knife
▌10- or 12-inch taping knife
▌120-grit sandpaper

Sometimes your project might call for taking out a window or door, or patching over a doorway to make a seamless wall. This calls for a large drywall patch. In projects like these, you'll need to frame the opening to provide sufficient backing for the patch and keep it from sagging between framing members, just as with ordinary drywall installation. For this application, space the framing 16 inches apart on-center, given that the patch needs as much support as possible. Make sure that the patch you install matches the thickness of the existing drywall. After fastening the patch, finish it using the customary tape (either paper or fiberglass mesh) and three-layer application of joint compound.

1 Prepare the opening. Remove the window or door and all the accompanying trimwork, and frame the opening with two-by lumber. If the existing wall contains insulation, install a comparable amount of insulation into the openings between the studs.

2 Install the new drywall piece. Measure, cut, and fasten in place a single piece of drywall that covers the opening.

3 Apply a bedding coat and tape. Apply a first coat of joint compound to the seams; then embed tape in the wet coat, and smooth it. Let this coat dry thoroughly.

4 Finish the joints. Scrape the first coat, and then apply a second coat of joint compound over the tape. Smooth it out, feathering the edges into the wall surface. Allow this coat to dry completely, and then knock down any burrs or high spots with a taping knife. Apply a third coat; let it dry; and then sand it to a finished smoothness.

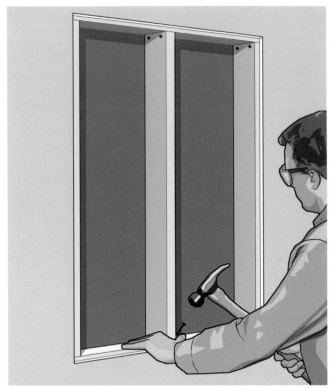

1 When a window (or door) is removed, frame up a structure that will serve to support a drywall patch.

3 Apply a layer of joint compound, and embed drywall tape into it while it is still wet.

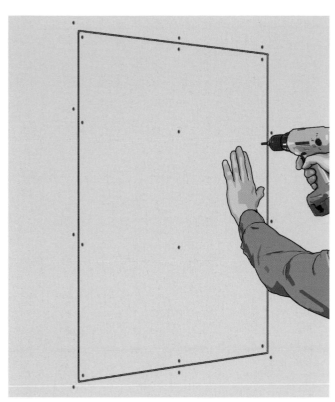

2 Cut and install a drywall patch by nailing or screwing around its edges where it rests on the framing members.

4 Finish the drywall joint as you would any drywall joint, with tape and a total of three coats of joint compound.

DRYWALL REPAIR KITS

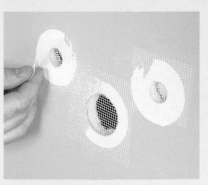

Repairing Small Holes. Kits include self-stick mesh patches that hold and reinforce the repair compound.

Covering the Mesh. The mesh patch keeps the compound from falling into the wall cavity.

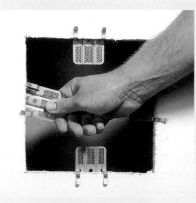

Patches for Large Holes. With clip kits. Set a clip on each side, and fasten it using a drywall screw.

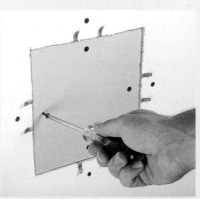

Adding Drywall. Fasten a drywall patch through each clip. Then you can snap off the exposed clip strips.

139

Repairing Drywall

Installing a Large Patch without the Need for Framing

Difficulty Level:

TOOLS & MATERIALS
▌ Framing square
▌ Utility knife
▌ 1x3 furring strips
▌ 1⅛-inch Type W drywall screws and screw gun
▌ Drywall
▌ Mesh or paper drywall tape
▌ Joint compound and taping knives
▌ 120-grit sandpaper

Occasionally you'll encounter a large hole that won't require structural framing to support the patch. In this case, you'll still want to attach furring strips to the back side of the drywall to serve as attachment backing. If the hole has an odd or ragged shape, start by trimming it to a square or rectangle. This will allow installation of a symmetrical piece of drywall. Make sure the patch's thickness is the same as that of the existing drywall.

1 Prepare the hole. Using a framing square as a guide, score around the rough hole with a utility knife to create a larger square or rectangular hole. Measure its dimensions.

2 Attach furring to the wall. Cut 1x3 furring strips that are 3 or 4 inches longer than the vertical measurement of the opening. Insert them into the opening, and then screw (with Type W drywall screws) through the surrounding drywall and into the furring strips to hold them in place. Install a furring strip at each side of the rough opening and at least one in the middle. Space them no more than 16 inches on center.

3 Install the drywall piece. Measure the perimeter of the hole, and cut a drywall patch to these measurements. Then fit this patch into the opening. Screw it to the furring strips, using at least two screws (one near each end) and additional screws every 6 or 7 inches.

4 Finish the joints. Apply a first coat of joint compound to the seams, and embed tape in the wet coat. Smooth this coat with a drywall knife, and then let it dry thoroughly. After scraping, apply a second layer of joint compound over the tape. Smooth it out, blending the edges into the wall surface. Let this coat dry, and then scrape it to remove burrs and high spots. Apply a third coat; allow it to dry; and then sand it.

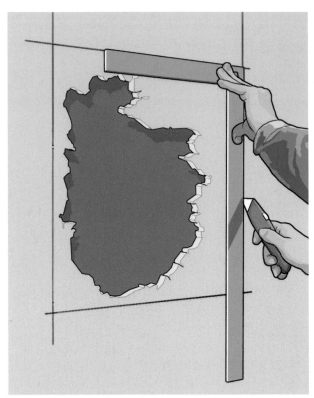

1 Ragged or asymmetrical holes need to be squared off. Cut a square or rectangle around the hole using a utility knife.

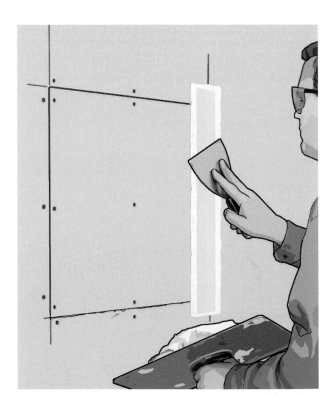

4 Finish the seams of the patch as you would any other seams, with paper or fiberglass mesh drywall tape and three coats of joint compound.

2 Install furring strips behind the wall, one on each end of the hole and one in the middle with a maximum on-center spacing of 16 in. Drive screws on each end of each furring strip.

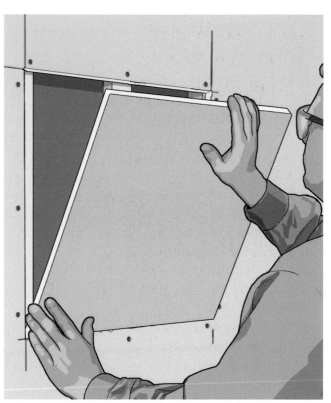

3 Install a drywall patch, and screw through it into the furring strips beneath.

PROVIDING SOLID NAILING

2x4 Studs

5⁄4x3 Blocking

2x4 Studs

Cut Line

Providing Nailing Surfaces. When a patch spans a full stud bay (left), studs need to be padded with blocking. These wood strips will act as a nailing or screwing base for a drywall patch and prevent it from sagging. If blocking is unavailable, cut down the midline of the studs with a utility knife to create a nailing surface for the patch (right). Be sure to locate and remove any fasteners before beginning the cut.

Repairing Drywall

FIXING A HOLE USING WIRE MESH

TO REPAIR SMALL HOLES without a wood-backed patch, you can use an old tradesman's trick. Thread one end of a 2-foot length of string through the center of a piece of sturdy wire mesh (known as hardware cloth). Tie that end of the string to a nail or small piece of wood to keep it from pulling through the mesh. Slip this mesh-and-string assembly into the hole, and pull the string taut so that the mesh presses against the inside of the surrounding drywall. While keeping tension on the string, apply joint compound. It will ooze through the mesh, holding it in place. After the first coat dries, cut off the string, and coat the patch as you would any small patch.

Mesh Patches. You can provide backing for a small patch by attaching a wood block to some wire mesh, inserting the mesh into the hole, and pulling on the string until the mesh is flush with the back of the drywall (top). Hold the string tight as you apply the joint compound (bottom).

FIXING A UTILITY-BOX OVERCUT

BECAUSE UTILITY BOXES ARE SMALL and so numerous in most drywalling jobs, it's quite likely that you will overcut the hole for at least a few of them, even if you use the coordinate method to position the hole. To fix an overcut hole, apply a layer of joint compound, squeezing it into the hole—some will stick to the utility box inside the wall and help support the patch. Cover this joint compound with paper or mesh tape, and then smooth more joint compound over the tape. After this layer has dried, follow it with two more coats of joint compound. Scrape any burrs or high spots between coats, and then finish-sand after the third coat has dried.

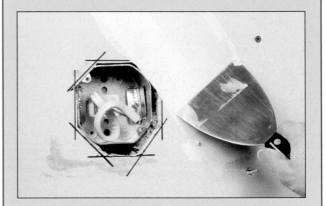

Fixing Measuring Errors. Cutouts for utility boxes are easy to miscalculate but fortunately just as easy to fix. (Note the large gap at the bottom of the box in the top photo.) Butt the straight edge of a piece of paper drywall tape up to the edge of the utility box for a clean, straight patch (bottom).

REPAIRING CORNER BEAD

OUTSIDE CORNERS, especially those located in high-traffic areas between rooms, are prone to damage. The metal corner bead that's typically installed in corners helps resist some damage, but at times an accident can be severe enough to warrant the replacement of the corner bead.

In most cases, it is best to remove only the damaged section of bead rather than the whole corner. Use a utility knife to trace around the damage. This will prevent you from tearing the paper on the drywall panel when you pry off the damaged section of bead. Cut through the metal guard using a hacksaw or

aviation snips. You will need a pry bar or the claw end of a hammer to pry the bead away from the wall.

Measure and cut a section of corner guard to replace the section you just removed. Install it using drywall screws or nails. Once the new section is in place, finish the corner with joint compound. Using the metal corner bead as a guide for your drywall knife, apply a thin coat to hide the bead. Apply a second coat when the first is dry. The trick with this repair is to feather the compound into the existing wall. Apply joint compound past the repaired section to help the patch blend in to the rest of the wall.

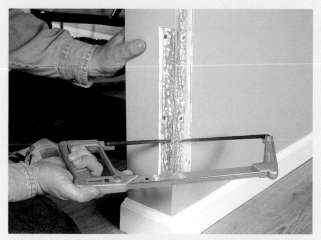

1 Remove the damaged bead. After outlining the damaged area, use a hacksaw to cut out the damaged bead.

2 Cut a corner bead patch. Using aviation snips, create a section of corner bead to replace the damaged one.

3 Install the corner bead. Use drywall screws or nails to hold the new corner guard in place, and make sure the flanges are below the wall surface.

4 Finish the repair using joint compound. Allow the raised edge of the corner bead to act as a guide for the taping knife as you apply the compound.

RESURFACING DRYWALL

SOMETIMES YOU MAY BE FACED WITH the problem of a wall that is too damaged to patch but not damaged enough to warrant demolishing the existing drywall and redoing the job. A situation like this may be caused by aging, water damage, or possibly numerous holes cut into a wall from an electrical or insulation job. Not only will making all these patches be time-consuming, but the odds are that the patchwork will still be visible once you've painted the walls. In this case, the best option to consider is drywall resurfacing.

Resurfacing has other advantages over patching besides the time saved: it offers the finished appearance of a brand-new surface. Resurfacing also gives you the opportunity of opening up framing cavities to install such items as new pipes, blown-in insulation, and electrical circuits. Also, if the walls of an older home are covered with layers of lead-based paint, you can skip the costly removal, as the health hazard, which is only made worse by sanding or scraping the lead, will be concealed under the new surface. Repainting could contain any lead hazard temporarily, but the risk would resurface, literally, any time in the future when repairs or improvements involved sanding or scraping into the old layers of lead paint.

The main drawback to resurfacing walls is the extra thickness. Thicker walls can be a problem where the new material meets trim. The margin between the wall surface and the surface of the trim creates a raised edge. In an older home the edge thickness around windows and doors is likely to be ¾ inch or more, but newer homes may have less than ½ inch. This is why you should opt for thinner ⅜- or even ¼-inch-thick panels when resurfacing.

While ¼-inch panels might seem like the best choice, many remodelers don't use them because they are fragile and too easy to break during construction. Slightly thicker ⅜-inch panels are often a better choice.

These final tips can help your resurfacing job go smoothly:
- Measure the total resurfacing area twice before ordering material.
- If you are re-covering old drywall, don't install new drywall panels with seams directly over old joints.
- Save installation and finishing time by applying construction adhesive to the backs of panels and securing them with Type G screws instead of nails. Properly driven, these fasteners will leave a neat dimple in the drywall surface that is easy to finish.

Resurfacing. Heavily damaged walls can be given a brand-new skin with a thin layer of new drywall, applied using construction adhesive and Type G drywall screws (left). An easy way to install the new panels by yourself is by using starter nails—a few stuck into the panel can be tapped in with one hand while you hold the panel with the other (right). The rest of the fasteners can be either nails or screws.

GETTING RID OF MOLD

MOLD CAN OCCUR INSIDE THE HOME when mold spores land on a wet surface. The wet surface can be caused by a leaky roof, flooding, or high levels of humidity, such as those found in an unvented bathroom. In many cases, small amounts of mold are harmless, but some people are extremely sensitive to molds and can suffer severe allergic reactions, such as sneezing, runny nose, red eyes, and skin rash. If you are one of these people, leave mold removal to a pro.

Molds can grow on many building products, and drywall is no exception. In an extremely wet area, such as an area around a tub that is not sealed properly, mold can grow in wall cavities. There have even been cases where mold spores thrived under wallpaper. In some cases, the only way you know you have a mold problem is due to the moldy smell in the room.

The first step in solving a mold problem is to correct whatever is causing the wet area. If you get rid of

the mold but don't correct the cause, the mold is sure to come back.

For small areas of mold, try cleaning with a household detergent. Wear gloves, and avoid breathing in the mold spores by working while wearing a N-95 respirator. It is best to seal off the room containing the mold so that spores do not travel to other areas during cleaning. Avoid running forced-air HVAC systems.

Severely moldy sections of drywall should be removed using one of the methods discussed earlier in this chapter. Place moldy drywall in heavy plastic bags, and dispose of the bags in accordance with your town's waste-management procedures. Leave large-scale mold problems to a pro.

Mold-Resistant Panels. Many manufacturers now offer mold-resistant drywall. This product is covered with a glass mat rather than paper to resist moisture and mold.

8 drywall projects

USING DRYWALL TECHNIQUES to add architectural or design touches to ceilings and walls can dramatically change the overall appearance of a home with a relatively small investment. You may have seen stunning effects, such as decorative soffit treatments or coffered ceilings, in a magazine or on a home-improvement show and thought that such projects were too advanced or expensive to try yourself. But features such as these can be accomplished using drywall and are well within the reach of the do-it-yourselfer.

SOFFIT DESIGN

Soffits have the ability to create two distinct but related impressions. First, the areas of lowered ceiling tend to convey a feeling of increased intimacy and purpose; for instance, a soffit can be used to define an area for a specific use, like a home office or TV nook. Second, by lowering the ceiling along the walls even a small amount, the ceiling in the rest of the room is perceived as being higher than it actually is—the contrast between the different ceiling heights can be an effective architectural tool, actually changing how you experience the room.

Soffits can be constructed to be any height and depth, and they needn't be used along all walls in a room or even the full length of a single wall. For example, while the project that begins on page 148 suggests the construction of a soffit around an entire room, you should feel free to use the same techniques to create a design that suits your own needs. This is one tool that gives you complete flexibility in deciding how you want to change your ceiling.

Practical Uses. In addition to modifying the shape of your ceiling, soffits provide a way to hide some pretty ugly mechanical items, such as pipes, ducts, and wires. While this is most often an issue in a basement or utility-room renovation, it can also come into play in the main rooms of a home, especially when new utilities are added to an older structure. For another option, you can add recessed lighting fixtures to a soffit—these can be tailored to a specific task, or they can provide ambient lighting for the room. While it would usually require cutting into the ceiling to run wires and install recessed fixtures, the soffit boxes allow you to easily add new lights with less mess and minimal disruption of the room at large.

One of the nice features of this type of project is that the materials required for construction are quite inexpensive. The framework for a soffit is usually built of 2x4 framing lumber or construction-grade plywood, and the finished surface is most often simple ½-inch-thick drywall. Of course, you have the option of applying other surface finishes to either the horizontal or vertical surfaces of a soffit; you could, for instance, apply wallpaper, boards, or tin ceiling panels to add another layer of detail or texture, or install a crown or bed molding at the points where the soffit joins the walls or ceiling.

Designs. The soffit in the basement ceiling shown below left hides pipes, ducts, and wires. In a media room, below right, the soffit style creates a cozy TV nook.

Drywall Projects

Some carpenters prefer to build soffits from construction-grade plywood and then sheath the surfaces with drywall. While this is certainly an acceptable approach, it can make it more difficult to run wires and install recessed light fixtures. To provide maximum flexibility, the alternative method is to assemble a framework of 2x2 and 2x4 lumber; this system allows you easy access to the interior of the soffit and makes it easy to add extra blocking to support hanging fixtures, if desired.

Before beginning actual construction, make a scale drawing of the room ceiling, including the new soffits. Use an electronic stud finder to locate the ceiling joists; mark the wall or ceiling adjacent to the intersecting walls to indicate the centerline of each joist.

The illustrated project includes the installation of recessed lighting fixtures—if you choose to install a soffit without any lighting, simply omit those steps.

Recessed Lights. To run electrical wiring within the soffit, assemble a framework using 2x2 and 2x4 lumber.

1 The vertical portion of the soffit is essentially a short 2x4 wall; the height equals the overall height of the soffit minus ½ in. (for drywall). For intersecting soffits, install double studs at the appropriate points to provide backing for the drywall at the inside corner and as a means of connecting the two soffit sections.

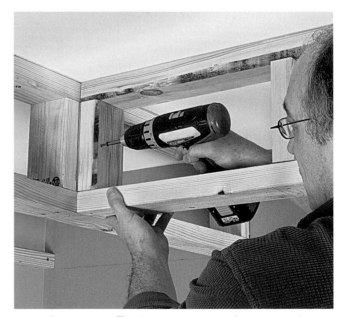

4 Where two soffits intersect, screw the two sections together to create a strong inside corner joint. Use a small "torpedo" level to check that the faces of the soffit sections remain plumb when you fasten them.

2 Establish chalk lines on the walls and ceiling to indicate the position of the outer edges of the soffit frame. These lines should be ½ in. inside the finished faces of the soffit to allow for the thickness of the drywall. Screw 2x2 blocking strips to the wall studs to form the back bottom edge of the soffit boxes. The distance from the ceiling to the bottom of these blocking strips should be equal to the height of the rough soffit faces.

3 Install the first soffit frame by screwing it to the ceiling joists. If your frame falls in a location where there are no joists, you can use hollow-wall anchors to hold the screws; for a small, lightweight soffit, spiral anchors will suffice, but for a large, heavy soffit, molly bolts or, better yet, toggle bolts are preferred.

5 Cut blocks of 2x4 lumber to form the bottom framework of the soffit. Mark the position of the blocks on the vertical soffit frames and on the blocking strips that are screwed to the wall. Toenail the blocks to both parts using 8d common nails. If you are planning to install recessed lighting fixtures in the soffit, make sure that the blocking does not interfere with the layout of the lights.

6 Once you have determined the desired spacing of the recessed light fixtures, mark those locations on the blocking strips and soffit face frames. Note: most fixtures are mounted on adjustable brackets that will span openings up to 24 in.; if your soffit is wider than that dimension, you will need to install additional blocking to support the lights. Nail or screw the mounting brackets to the soffit framing. Continued on next page.

Continued from previous page.

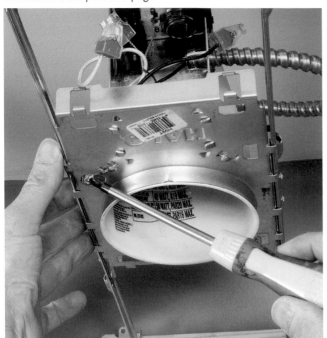

7 After you have fastened the lights to the soffit, you can still slide the fixture along the mounting rails. Move the body into the desired position, double-checking by measuring from the wall to the center of the fixture opening; then tighten the screw provided to lock it in place.

8 Run the wiring between fixtures before connecting the house wiring. You will have one wire bringing power into the fixture and another carrying power out to the next light. If you're using nonmetallic cable, you can place both wires through the same connector. Remove 4 or 5 in. of sheathing, and strip the wires to expose about $\frac{1}{2}$ in. of the copper core. Tighten the screws on the connector to fix the cables to the junction box.

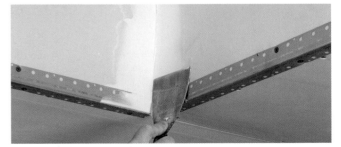

11 Lift the drywall panel into position, and fasten it to the soffit framing using drywall screws. Set the clutch on your drill-driver so that the screwheads are set just below the surface of the drywall, creating a small dimple. Drive screws every 8 in. along the edges of the panel and into the intermediate blocking.

12 Install metal corner bead on all outside soffit edges (top). Use drywall screws to attach the bead to the framing. Cut the strips to length using metal shears. To finish an inside corner, begin by using a 3-in. drywall knife to spread compound on both surfaces (bottom).

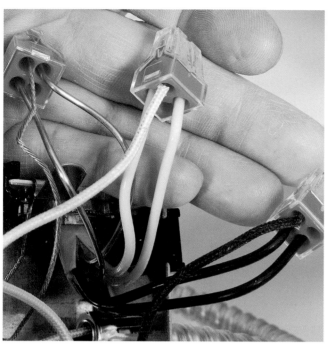

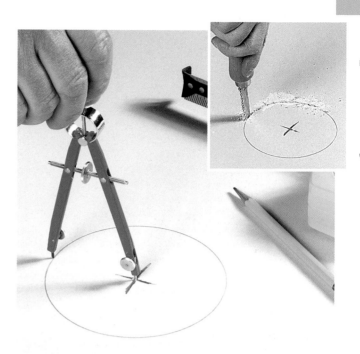

9 These fixtures use "push-in" connectors, which eliminate the need for wire nuts. Simply push the exposed ends of the wires into the appropriate connector until it locks in place. Connect white wires to white wires, black wires to black wires, and copper ground connectors to each other. If you are not experienced in electrical work, hire an electrician to check your rough wiring and connect the circuits to the main house wiring.

10 Cut the drywall panels to cover the bottom surface of the soffit. If you have recessed lights in the soffit, carefully measure the locations of the center of each light, and transfer those dimensions to the drywall panel. Set a compass to draw a circle that is ¼ in. larger in diameter than the actual lights, and mark the outline of the cutouts on the drywall. Use a drywall saw to cut the openings for recessed light fixtures (inset).

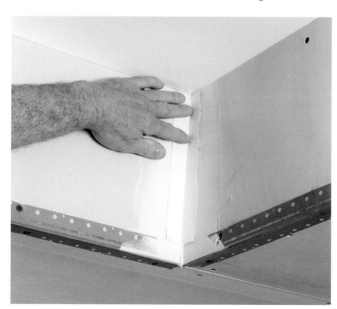

13 Cut a piece of drywall tape to length, and fold it lengthwise down the center to create a crease. Gently embed the tape into the compound; then use the drywall knife to smooth the tape. Cover one side of the tape with compound, and let it dry overnight before coating the second side. Lightly sand when dry. (See Chapter 6, "Taping and Finishing," page 106.)

14 Install trim for light fixtures by pushing it into the housing until the clips snap into place. You will find a great selection of trim ring styles, allowing you to tailor the look of the fixtures to suit your decor.

151

Drywall Projects

Creating a Coffered Ceiling Using Drywall

Difficulty Level: 🐟🐟🐟

TOOLS & MATERIALS

▪ Chalk line ▪ Cordless screw driver
▪ Drywall screwgun ▪ 3-inch drywall screws
▪ 1¼-inch drywall screws ▪ 2-inch drywall screws
▪ Utility knife ▪ Caulk gun
▪ Drywall adhesive ▪ ½-inch drywall
▪ 2x4 lumber ▪ Adhesive caulk (paintable)
▪ Tray ceiling bead ▪ L-bead
▪ Staple gun and ½-inch staples
▪ Spray adhesive ▪ Plastic laminate
▪ Joint compound ▪ 3-inch taping knife
▪ Fiberglass mesh drywall joint tape
▪ Mud pan for holding compound
▪ Variety of decorative corner beads
▪ Miter saw, tin snips ▪ Acoustical wall covering
▪ Heavy duty wallpaper paste ▪ Wallpaper brush
▪ Paint roller (½-inch nap) ▪ Sanding pad, 200 grit

Thanks to the availability of a variety of drywall corner and edge beads, you can use standard drywall to create decorative effects, such as the coffered ceiling shown here.

Coffered Ceiling. The treatment in this home theater creates a feeling of luxury and expansiveness.

1 Build a 5½-in.-deep soffit around the perimeter of the room. Create a design for the coffers, and snap chalk lines for the layout. You could construct a full-scale model of the coffers to see how the final design will look. Rip 2x4s to 1¾ in. wide to use as furring. Attach the furring using 3-in. drywall screws. If you can't attach to a ceiling joist, attach drywall using construction adhesive and screws. You can remove the screws once the adhesive takes hold.

4 Cut the bead using a sharp pair of snips. Hold the piece in the corner of the coffer, and make adjustments in the cut if necessary before attaching the bead.

2 Cut drywall to width, and attach it to furring using screws. To install the angled tray ceiling bead, you will need to lower the ceiling by 2½ in., so install a second layer of ½-in. drywall over the first. Make this strip 2 in. wide. This edge will be covered with a decorative bead.

3 The vinyl bead used to create the angled edges of the coffered ceiling is called EZ-Tray, and it is manufactured by Trim-Tex. Join the edges where they meet in the corners using miter cuts. Use a miter-marking tool that comes with the bead to mark out the angle You can miter all the joints, or you can square cut one side of the angle and miter the other.

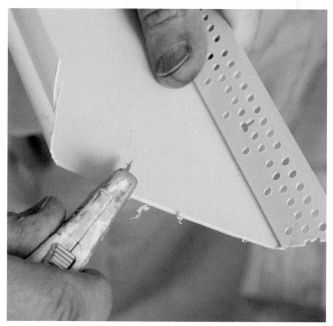

5 Fine tune the fit using a sharp utility knife. In this photo the back edge is being beveled so it will fit tightly against the bead already attached with the square end cut.

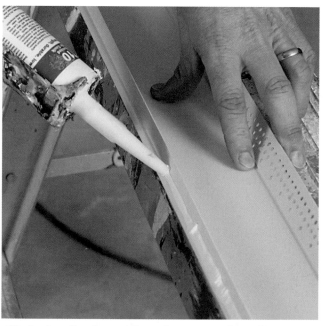

6 Apply adhesive caulk to the groove along the upper edge of the part of the bead that will fit against the ceiling. You may need to touch up this area with painter's caulk before painting. For best results, do the follow-up caulking after priming. Continued on next page.

Continued from previous page.

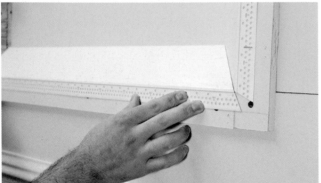

7 Apply two thin coats of spray-on contact adhesive to the drywall. Then line up the mud-flange edge of the bead to a snapped chalk line on the drywall. Press the bead in place, and use ½-in. staples spaced every 12 in. along the flange edge. Apply joint compound to cover the flange after the adhesive dries.

8 You could simply paint the 2-in. wide area between the "beams." Another option is to apply a decorative plastic laminate. Use the same contact cement you used on the tray bead flange to hold the laminate in place.

11 You will be left with a 2-in.-wide area that needs to be covered with joint compound. Usually just two coats of compound are all that is needed. Follow by sanding with a fine sanding sponge. Then prime with a latex drywall primer, and seal edges with painters caulk. Priming prior to caulking results in cleaner looking edges.

12 For sound control if desired, attach a paintable acoustical wallcovering to the ceiling between the "beam" sections. It consists of a foam backing with a decorative fiberglass face. Cut each piece a little large for the area to be covered. You can trim the excess after application as you would when applying wallpaper.

9 For the remaining exposed edge, cut the bead using a power miter saw equipped with a fine-tooth blade. Lower the blade slowly to help prevent any chipping of the bead. To get accurate angle cuts that fit together perfectly, support the flange-edge of the bead with a ½-in.-thick section of drywall.

10 Attach the decorative L-bead over the exposed ½-in. strip of drywall. Use the same spray adhesive used to attach the EZ-Tray. It is usually not necessary to use the adhesive caulk to hold the outer edge in place, although caulk is typically used later (after priming) to blend in this edge.

13 Apply a heavy-duty vinyl wallcovering adhesive to the ceiling. Then position and brush the acoustical wallcovering into place using a wallpaper brush just as you would with a traditional wallcovering. Trim to fit the area. Other finishing options include hand- or spray-applied texture finishes.

14 The finished look is incredible. It is amazing that this coffer was created using scrap drywall, wood furring, and decorative corner bead.

Drywall Projects

Creating a Media Center Using Drywall

Difficulty Level: 🐟🐟🐟

TOOLS & MATERIALS

▌2x6 lumber ▌Chalk-line box
▌½-in. drywall ▌Drywall screwgun
▌1¼-, 2-inch drywall screws ▌Utility knife
▌⅜-inch bullnose cornerbeads and
other decorative beads
▌Spray adhesive contact cement
▌Adhesive caulk, gun ▌Spray adhesive
▌Power miter saw or tin snips
▌Staple gun and ½-in. staples
▌Sanding pad (200 grit) ▌2x4 lumber
▌Scoring tool (Blade Runner)
▌Drywall joint compound
▌Paper joint tape ▌6-inch taping knife
▌Mud pan, trowel ▌Paintbrush, paint

You can create some custom looks using layered drywall and corner beads. This project is a drywall media center flanked by drywall "curtains."

Wall Unit. Drywall "curtains" create a frame for a flat-screen TV alcove.

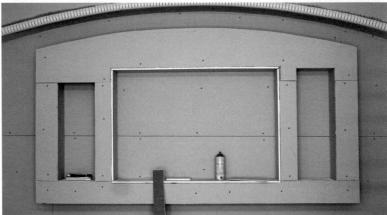

1 Build a shallow frame that will hold a flat-screen TV and two side shelf areas (top) by first constructing three boxes using 2x6s set on edge. Join the boxes, creating one unit, using 2x6s face out. The facing creates a recessed edge. Determine where you want the frame to be, and screw 2x4 cleats to the wall to secure the frame at the top and bottom. Cover the frame with drywall (bottom). Here, the top edge was shaped to match the arch above. (The left alcove is still untrimmed.)

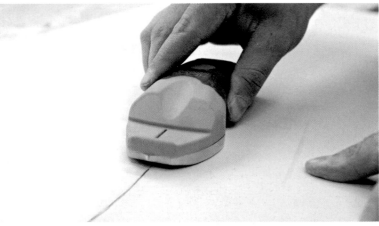

4 Cut drywall so that the edges are curved. A special tool with a magnetic top and bottom scores both the front and back of the drywall. Simply follow the line with the tool (called a Blade Runner), and snap the waste piece loose. Install three layers, cutting each layer to create a random look, which will appear more natural.

2 Attach ⅜-in. bullnose corner bead to the edges of the framework using spray adhesive and staples spaced every 12 in. The best way to cut the bead is with a miter saw. The rounded edge used here complements the other corner bead in the room and will stand up to more abuse than a square-edge bead. Apply three coats of compound followed by sanding with a 200-grit sanding pad.

3 For an added touch, create false "curtains" made using layered drywall attached to a wooden frame. This "ladder" frame consists of ripped 2x4s from the ceiling project on page 152 and 6-in.-wide 2x6 blocking. Attach three layers of progressively more-narrow drywall strips, shaped to resemble pulled-back curtains, using drywall adhesive and ½-in. longer screws with each layer.

5 Cover the edges of the drywall with flexible L-bead. Attach the bead using spray adhesive and ½-in.-long staples spaced every 12 in. or more if necessary. Conceal the mud flange with at least two coats of drywall joint compound, sanding between coats.

6 You can simply paint the freeform-shaped "curtains," or add texture to enhance the look and bring the design to life. One option is to apply thinned-out joint compound using a paintbrush before painting. This texture treatment will give the finished "curtains" the look of fabric.

157

Drywall Projects

Planning the Layout For Wall Tiles

Difficulty Level:

TOOLS & MATERIALS
▌ Layout board and marker
▌ Level
▌ Chalk-line box
▌ Tape measure

Ceramic tile is a great wall finish for damp or wet areas like kitchens and bathrooms. And it's a frequent choice for laundry rooms and mudrooms. When properly installed, it's impervious to water and provides another design texture that livens up just about any room. Even though tiling a wall can be time consuming, it's not difficult work. One big reason: adhesives that are formulated to hold the tiles in place while the adhesives are still wet. Here are the steps required for laying out tile that will be installed on drywall. Follow by installing tile.

1 Prepare a layout board by marking lines on the face and edge that match the size of your tiles plus the grout joint. Then hold the board against the center of the wall, and transfer the layout marks to the wall.

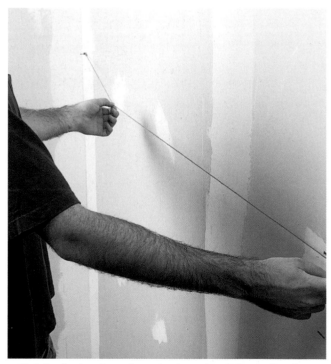

4 Join the level marks at both ends of the wall using a chalk line. Drive a small nail in both marks; then hang one end of the chalk line to one nail. Wrap the other end around the second nail, and pull it tight. Then snap the string in the middle to leave a clear line.

5 Use your layout board to mark the tile increments on the chalk line. Then use a level to establish plumb marks at the top and bottom of the wall. The logical place to make this line is next to your layout marks.

2 When the layout reaches the ceiling, check the distance between the last mark and the ceiling to find out what size tile will fit in this space. A piece that's at least as big as half a tile will look best. If you wind up with a small piece, split the difference with the bottom row of tile at the floor.

3 Once you have established the final tile layout between the floor and ceiling, determine the layout from side to side. To do this, use a 4-ft. level to carry one of the layout lines to both ends of the wall. Do this in several steps, or just hold the level on top of a long straight board that spans the whole wall.

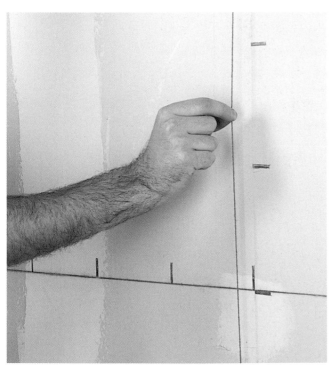

6 As you did with the horizontal guideline, drive nails through the plumb marks at the top and bottom of the wall. Then hang a chalk line on these nails, and snap a clean line. Use the same process to establish other guidelines you may need for trim pieces.

7 Before starting to install the tile, mark the location on the floor of any important framing fixtures that are hidden behind the drywall. Examples are reinforcement blocks for grab bars, towel racks, or other specialized fixtures that you plan to hang on the finished wall.

Fire Ratings

Fire-resistance ratings are given in hours; each number represents an hour that this construction will contain a fire and give protection from it under laboratory conditions. Sound transmission class (STC) ratings are given by the ASTM for sound-attenuating performance with regard to speech (not as accurate for mechanical noise, music, or other low-frequency sounds). The figure given is the minimum STC rating.

FIRE RATING	STC	DESCRIPTION	WALL SECTION
1 hour	30	Veneer plaster (approx. $\frac{3}{32}$ in.) on gypsum lath subbase ($\frac{1}{2}$ in.) on both sides of a 2×4 stud wall 16 in. o.c.	Plaster / Lath / 16" O.C.
1 hour	35	One layer $\frac{5}{8}$-in. Type X drywall on both sides of a 2×4 stud wall 16 in. o.c.	$\frac{5}{8}$" Type X Drywall / 16" O.C.
1 hour	35	One layer $\frac{5}{8}$-in. Type X drywall on both sides of a $1\frac{5}{8}$-in. metal stud wall 24 in. o.c.	$\frac{5}{8}$" Type X Drywall / $1\frac{5}{8}$" Metal Stud / 24" O.C.
1 hour	40	One layer $\frac{5}{8}$-in. Type X drywall on both sides of a $3\frac{5}{8}$-in. metal stud wall 24 in. o.c.	$\frac{5}{8}$" Type X Drywall / $3\frac{5}{8}$" Metal Stud / 24" O.C.
1 hour	45	One layer of $\frac{5}{8}$-in. Type X drywall attached over one layer of $\frac{1}{2}$-in. fiberboard on both sides of a 2×4 stud wall 16 in. o.c.	16" O.C. / $\frac{5}{8}$" Type X Drywall / $\frac{1}{2}$" Fiberboard
1 hour	45	Two layers $\frac{5}{8}$-in. Type X drywall on one side, and one layer on the other side of a $3\frac{5}{8}$-in. metal stud wall 24 in. o.c. with $3\frac{1}{2}$ in. of fiberglass insulation in cavity	$\frac{5}{8}$" Type X Drywall / Fiberglass Insulation / 24" O.C. / 2 Layers $\frac{5}{8}$" Type X Drywall / $3\frac{5}{8}$" Metal Stud

FIRE RATING	STC	DESCRIPTION	WALL SECTION
1 hour	50	One layer ⅝-in. Type X drywall on both sides of a 2×4 stud wall 16 in. o.c., one side installed on resilient metal hat channel, with 1½ in. of mineral fiber insulation in wall cavity	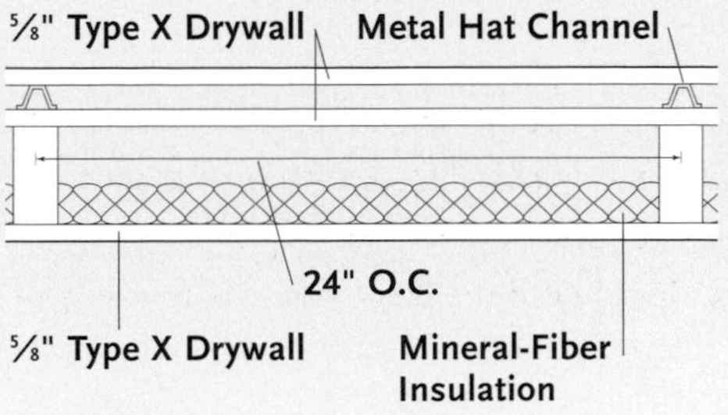 ⅝" Type X Drywall — Metal Hat Channel — 24" O.C. — ⅝" Type X Drywall — Mineral-Fiber Insulation
2 hours	50	Two layers ⅝-in. Type X drywall on both sides of a 2×4 stud wall framed 16 in. o.c.	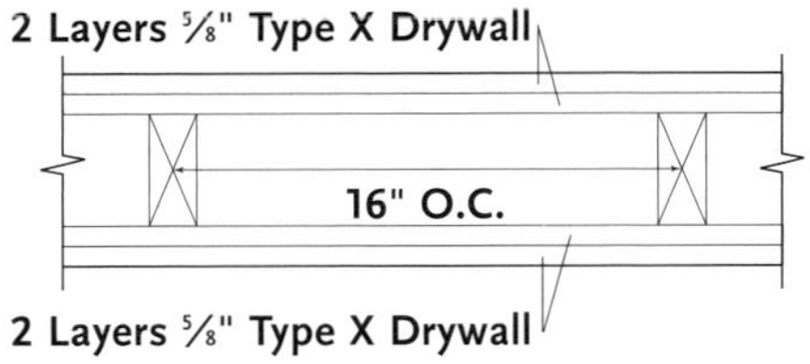 2 Layers ⅝" Type X Drywall — 16" O.C. — 2 Layers ⅝" Type X Drywall
2 hours	50	Two layers ⅝-in. Type X drywall on both sides of a stud wall with staggered 2×4s, 8 in. o.c., on 2×6 plates	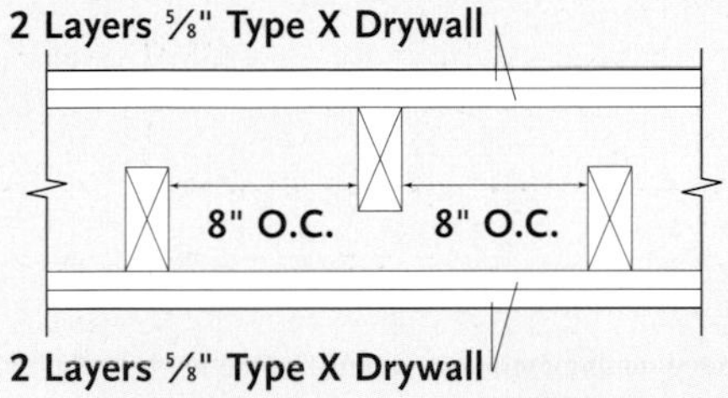 2 Layers ⅝" Type X Drywall — 8" O.C. — 8" O.C. — 2 Layers ⅝" Type X Drywall
2 hours	55	Two layers ⅝-in. Type X drywall on both sides of a stud wall with a double row of 2×4s, 16 in. o.c., on separate plates 1 in. apart, with 3½ in. of fiberglass insulation in wall cavity, and GWB fire stop in space between plates	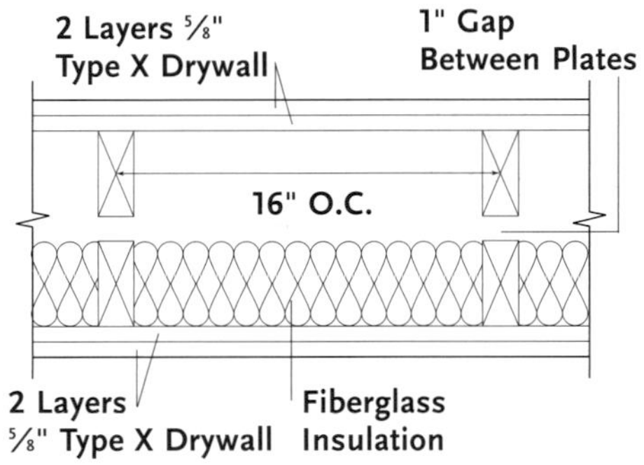 2 Layers ⅝" Type X Drywall — 1" Gap Between Plates — 16" O.C. — 2 Layers ⅝" Type X Drywall — Fiberglass Insulation
2 hours	55	2 layers ⅝-in. Type X drywall on both sides of 3⅝-in. metal studs 24 in. o.c.; one side has ¼ or ⅜-in. prefinished panels or laminating compound; 3½ in. of fiberglass insulation in cavity	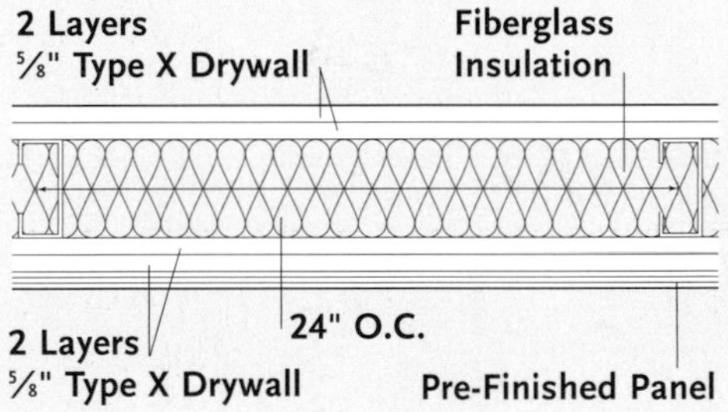 2 Layers ⅝" Type X Drywall — Fiberglass Insulation — 2 Layers ⅝" Type X Drywall — 24" O.C. — Pre-Finished Panel
3 hours	45	¾ × 24-in. prefinished Type X drywall installed between 2¼-in. metal I-studs; other side has base layer of ⅝-in. Type X drywall perpendicular to studs, a 2nd layer of ⅝-in. Type X parallel to studs, a 3rd layer of ⅝-in. Type X parallel to studs, and then hat channel 24 in. o.c. perpendicular to studs, with 4th layer of ⅝-in. Type X perpendicular to channels, with 1-in. fiberglass insulation behind channels	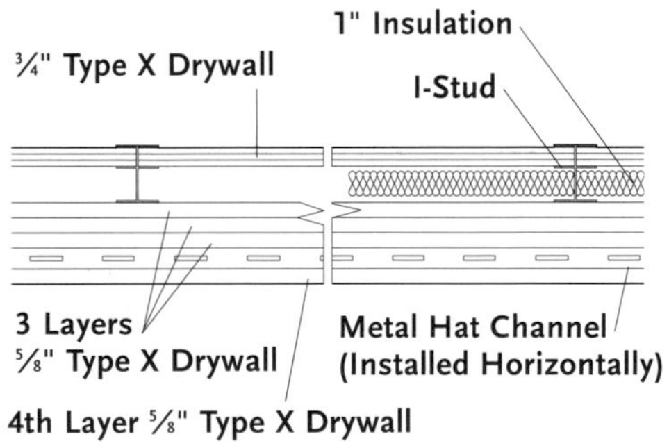 ¾" Type X Drywall — 1" Insulation — I-Stud — 3 Layers ⅝" Type X Drywall — Metal Hat Channel (Installed Horizontally) — 4th Layer ⅝" Type X Drywall

Recommended Levels for Drywall Finish

Four industry associations—*The Association of the Wall and Ceiling Industries International, The Gypsum Association, Ceiling and Interior Systems Construction Association,* and *Painting and Decorating Contractors of America*—have established a guide to drywall finishing based on the final decoration of the wall or ceiling. Here are the minimum requirements for each type of decoration.

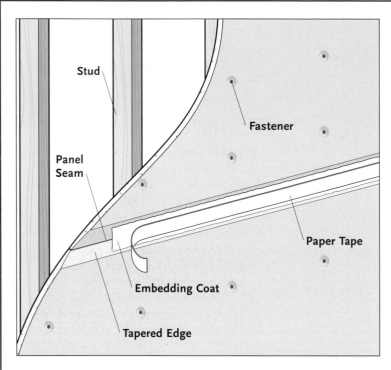

LEVEL 1

All joints and interior angles shall have tape set in joint compound. Surface shall be free of excess joint compound. Tool marks and ridges are acceptable.

Frequently specified in plenum areas above ceilings, in attics, and in areas where the assembly would generally be concealed. Some degree of sound and smoke control is provided; in some geographic areas, this level is referred to as "firetaping." Where a fire-resistance rating is required for the gypsum board assembly, details of construction shall be in accordance with reports of fire tests of assemblies that have met the fire-rating requirement. Tape and fastener heads need not be covered with joint compound.

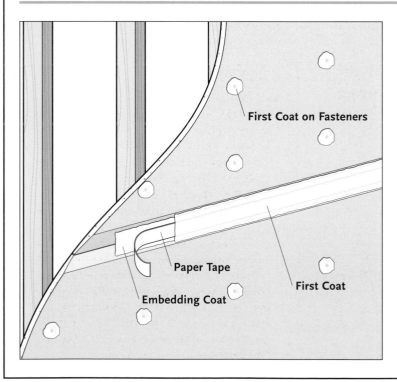

LEVEL 2

All joints and interior angles shall have tape embedded in joint compound and wiped with a joint knife leaving a thin coating of joint compound over all joints and interior angles. Fastener heads and accessories shall be covered with one coat of joint compound. Surface shall be free of excess joint compound. Tool marks and ridges are acceptable. Joint compound applied over the body of the tape at the time of tape embedment shall be considered a separate coat of joint compound and shall satisfy the conditions of this level.

Specified where water-resistant gypsum backing board (ASTM C 630) is used as a substrate for tile; may be specified in garages or other similar areas where surface appearance is not of primary concern.

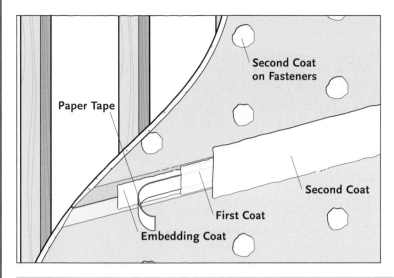

LEVEL 3

Same requirements as Level 2 with one additional coat of joint compound applied over all joints, interior angles, and fastener heads. All joint compound shall be smooth and free of tool marks and ridges. **Note:** It is recommended that the prepared surface be coated with a drywall primer prior to the application of final finishes.

Typically specified in appearance areas which are to receive heavy- or medium-texture (spray or hand-applied) finishes before final painting, or where heavy grade wallcoverings are to be applied. This level of finish is not recommended where smooth painted surfaces or light-to-medium wallcoverings are specified.

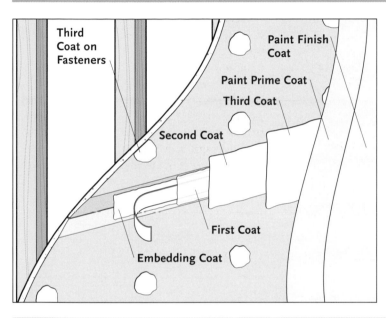

LEVEL 4

Same requirements as Level 3 with an additional coat of compound applied over all flat joints and fastener heads. An additional coat of compound over interior angles is not required. All joint compound shall be smooth and free of tool marks and ridges. **Note:** It is recommended that the prepared surface be coated with a drywall primer prior to the application of final finishes.

This level should be specified where flat paints, light textures, or wallcoverings are to be applied. In critical lighting areas, flat paints applied over light textures tend to reduce joint photographing. Gloss, semigloss, and enamel paints are not recommended over this level of finish. Unbacked vinyl wallcoverings are not recommended over this level of finish.

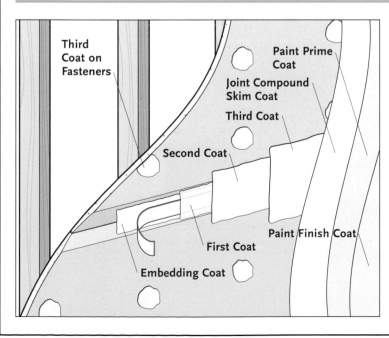

LEVEL 5

All joints, interior angles, and fasteners shall follow the requirements specified in Level 4. In addition, a thin skim coat of joint compound, or a material manufactured especially for this purpose, shall be applied to the entire surface. The surface shall be smooth and free of tool marks and ridges. **Note:** It is recommended that the prepared surface be coated with a drywall primer prior to the application of finish paint.

This level of finish is highly recommended where gloss, semigloss, enamel, or nontextured flat paints are specified or where severe lighting conditions occur. This highest quality finish is the most effective method to provide a uniform surface and minimize the possibility of joint photographing and of fasteners showing through the final decoration.

Resource Guide

This list of manufacturers and associations is meant to be a general guide to additional industry and product-related sources. It is not intended as a listing of products and manufacturers represented by the photographs in this book.

MANUFACTURERS, DISTRIBUTORS, AND RETAILERS

Apla-Tech
W2024 Industrial Dr. #3
Kaukauna WI 54130
800-827-3721
www.apla-tech.com
Manufactures pneumatic and continuous-flow drywall finishing tools.

Columbia Tools
1-5508 Production Blvd.
Surrey, B.C. V3S8P5
Canada
800-663-8121
www.columbiatools.com
Manufactures taping tools and accessories.

Dura-Stilts
800-225-2440
www.durastilt.com
Offers a variety of professional stilts. Visit the company's Web site to view products and product manuals.

EZRip
P.O. Box 1566
Vallejo, CA 94590
707-552-5510
www.buyezrip.com
Manufactures the EZRip drywall-cutting tool. The company's Web site offers testimonials, warranty information, and detailed information about the product.

FibaTape, a div. of Saint-Gobain Technical Fabrics
345 Third St., Ste. 615
Niagara Falls, NY 14303
www.fibatape.com
Manufactures sanding and drywall products.

Flannery, Inc.
300 Parkside Dr.
San Fernando, CA 91340
818-837-7585
www.flannerytrim.com
Manufactures specialty drywall and plaster trim.

Georgia-Pacific
133 Peachtree St., NE
Atlanta, GA 30303
404-652-4000
www.gp.com
Manufactures building products and related chemicals. Visit the company's Web site to view its Education Station.

Goldblatt Taping Tools
15785 S. Keeler Ter.
Olathe, KS 66062
877-876-7562
www.goldblatttapingtools.com
Manufacturers a full range of drywall tools, including the Blade Runner drywall cutter.

National Gypsum
2001 Rexford Rd.
Charlotte, NC 28211
704-365-7300
www.nationalgypsum.com
Manufactures and supplies building and construction products. The company's Web site features resources for do-it-yourselfers and professionals.

Phillips Manufacturing Co.
4949 S. 30th St.
Omaha, NE 68107
800-822-5055
www.phillipsmfg.com
Designs and manufactures custom drywall and metal and vinyl trim and beads.

Pittcon Industries
6409 Rhode Island Ave.
Riverdale, MD 20737
www.pittconindustries.com
Manufactures decorative drywall panels. Visit the company's Web site for an exhibition of its projects.

Trim-Tex
3700 W. Pratt Ave.
Lincolnwood, IL 60712
800-874-2333
www.trim-tex.com
Manufactures and distributes vinyl drywall beads and drywall finishing accessories. The company's Web site features a full catalog, as well as a gallery of projects using Trim-Tex products.

USG
www.usg.com
Manufactures and supplies building materials. The company's Web site features its history, product information, and a resource guide.

Vinyl Corp.
8000 NW 79th Pl.
Miami, FL 33166
800-648-4695
www.vinylcorp.com
Manufactures vinyl beads, trim, and control joints.

West-Tech
#203 – 20628 Mufford Cres.
Langley, BC V2Y 1N8
Canada
604-534-0044
www.westtechtools.com
Manufactures taping tools and parts and accessories. You can purchase the company's products directly through its Web site.

ASSOCIATIONS

Association of the Wall and Ceilings Industries (AWCI)
803 W. Broad St., Ste. 600
Falls Church, VA 22046
703-534-8300
www.awci.org
Provides services and offers information for individuals and businesses in the drywall and ceiling industries. The association's Web site offers an online buyers' guide, and a page of helpful links for do-it-yourselfers and professionals.

The Ceilings & Interior Systems Construction Association (CISCA)
1500 Lincoln Hwy., Ste. 202
St. Charles, IL 60174
630-584-1919
www.cisca.org
Promotes the interests of the interior commercial trade industry. The association's Web site offers educational materials and resources.

Gypsum Association
810 First St. NE, Ste. 510
Washington, DC 20002
202-289-5440
www.gyspum.org
Promotes the gypsum industry in the United States and Canada. The Web site provides articles, publications, educational information, and industry statistics.

Glossary

Abuse-resistant drywall A heavy-duty type of drywall—available in $\frac{1}{2}$- and $\frac{5}{8}$-inch thicknesses—that has heavier paper than regular panels and a reinforced core.

Arc Any portion of a circle, such as those found in an archway or curved wall.

Arch bead A plastic or metal strip designed to finish curved drywall seams in arched doorways or windows.

ASTM Formerly the American Society for Testing and Materials, now known by the initials; a nonprofit organization that publishes standards for various materials.

Backer board See *Cement board.*

Backing A stable surface to which a drywall panel can be nailed—either the framing members of the house, extra members that have been added, nailer blocks, or drywall clips.

Beveled edge See *Tapered edge.*

Beveled trowel Used for wide-coat applications, this tool resembles a mason's finishing trowel and has a slight bow so that it leaves a barely perceptible crown in the center of a coat of joint compound.

Blocking Lumber added between studs, joists, rafters, or other framing members to provide a nailing surface for sheathing or drywall.

Blown ceiling Popcorn-like texturing material fed through a hopper to an airless spray gun and blown onto a ceiling, where it is left to dry.

Blue board See *Moisture-resistant drywall.*

Boom truck A truck with an articulated crane arm that can lift drywall to a second-story window.

Brocade A textured finish made by pressing a flat metal or wooden hand trowel into wet joint compound and quickly pulling it away.

Cement board Also called backer board and cementitious panel, this material is made with a portland cement core reinforced with polymer-coated glass fiber mesh embedded in both faces. Used as a substrate for tiles in wet areas.

Cement-coated nails Smooth-shanked nails coated with cement to increase resistance to withdrawal.

Chalk-line box A tool with a length of chalk-coated twine that is pulled taut across the face of a drywall panel or other surface and snapped to mark a straight line.

Circle cutter A tool used to make circular cutouts. The hand-operated type has a center pin through which slides an L-shaped arm with a cutting edge that you adjust to the desired radius.

Contact cement An adhesive used to attach vinyl-faced panels to a drywall base.

Cooler nails Smooth-shanked drywall nails.

Corner bead A length of thin-gauge galvanized-steel angle with holes drilled in its flanges, which is used to reinforce and protect an outside drywall corner.

Corner crimper A device used to set corner bead in place without nails. Hitting it with a mallet crimps the edges of the corner bead, setting metal burrs into the drywall panels that hold it in place.

Corner knife A two-faced knife that forms an inside corner and is used to finish corner seams.

Corner tape Flexible paper tape with 1-inch-wide galvanized-metal reinforcement used on outside and inside corners that form an angle greater than 90 degrees.

Deadman Also called a T-support or T-brace, this wooden device consists of a short cross brace at the end of a support that is slightly longer than the ceiling is high. It is used to pin and hold a drywall ceiling panel in place until it is fastened.

Drywall adhesive A product used to fasten drywall panels to wood or metal studs, or directly to concrete, masonry, or old drywall.

Drywall clips L-shaped metal braces measuring about 2 inches wide, which are used to attach partition walls to framing that provides insufficient backing.

Drywall hammer A hammer with a convex-faced head on one end and a tapered edge on the other. The rounded head creates a dimple in the drywall that can be neatly filled with joint compound. The tapered edge can be used to pry drywall panels in place.

Drywall jack Also called a panel lift, this caster-mounted tool is used to cradle a drywall panel, wheel it into position, crank it to the desired height, and hold it snugly in place for fastening.

Drywall nails Three types are available: ringed nails, cement-coated nails, and cooler nails, each of which has a minimum head diameter of $\frac{1}{4}$ inch.

Drywall saw A short, stout handsaw used to make long, straight cuts in drywall panels.

Drywall screws Three general types are available: Type W (for wood), Type G (for gypsum), and Type S (for steel).

Drywall tape Made from paper or fiberglass, it is applied to drywall seams or cracks as a base for joint compound.

Dust barrier A polyethylene sheet stapled or taped over an entry to prevent the escape of construction dust.

Dust-mist respirator A mask for the nose and mouth that filters out dust through a replaceable filter cartridge.

End-butt joint A seam where nontapered drywall panel ends or cut edges meet.

Factory edge See *Tapered edge.*

Fascia The vertical area between the wall-ceiling joint and the soffit.

Feathering The process of laying down a wide, thin layer of joint compound over a seam and sanding it gradually into the wallboard at the edges so that the mound of compound seems flat.

Fiberglass tape Also called mesh tape, this netlike material is adhered to a dry seam (with staples or its own adhesive) and then followed with a first coat of joint compound.

Filler coat The middle or second coat of joint compound in a three-coat application.

Finish coat The final coat of joint compound.

Fire-resistant drywall A type of drywall with a fiberglass-reinforced core that meets or exceeds the ASTM C36 rating for Type X fire-resistant gypsum board.

Fire wall A wall made with a type of ⅝-inch-thick drywall that contains fire-retardant material.

Flexible bead L-shaped vinyl material used to finish a curved drywall edge, as in an archway or above a curved window.

Flexible drywall Drywall panels, ¼ inch thick, which are specially designed to withstand bending.

Foil-backed board Drywall laminated with aluminum foil (backed by kraft paper) to increase the drywall's insulation value and its effectiveness as a vapor barrier.

Framing members The structural elements of the house framework, consisting of studs, joists, plates, rafters, and so on.

Furring Softwood or stainless-steel strips, usually 2½ inches wide and ⅝ or 1 inch thick (depending on desired stand-off), which are attached to studs or existing walls to create a flat backing for drywall panels.

Ghosting See *Photographing.*

Green board See *Moisture-resistant drywall.*

Gypsum A mineral (calcium sulfate) that, after processing, forms the core of drywall panels.

Hawk A wide, flat aluminum tray with a short handle used to hold joint compound.

Jab saw See *Utility saw.*

J-bead Edge-finishing material that wraps around the edge of a drywall panel to protect it from damage or disintegration; used where a drywall panel abuts a brick wall, a window jamb, or a shower stall. Finishing-type J-bead has a front flange that requires joint compound; reveal-type has a factory finish and is not meant to be used with joint compound.

Joint compound A plaster-like substance used to fill seams and irregularities in drywalling, either the vinyl-based drying type, which hardens as the water medium dries, or setting type, which hardens by a chemical reaction that is catalyzed by water.

Joist Framing lumber placed horizontally on edge, to which subfloors or ceilings are attached.

Laminating adhesive A product designed to adhere layers of drywall in double-layer applications, and to attach drywall to concrete or rigid foam insulation (polystyrene or urethane).

Lath 1½ × ⅜-inch-thick softwood strips that are nailed to studs to serve as backing for plaster.

L-bead Edge-finishing material used on a panel that abuts a door or window casing that isn't designed to cover a drywall edge.

Load-bearing That part of a structure that supports the weight of the structure above it. Load-bearing walls are perpendicular to the rafters and joists.

Mixing paddle A tool used to blend fresh joint compound.

Moisture-resistant drywall Also called blue board or green board; a moisture-resistant (not waterproof) type of wallboard that can withstand high levels of humidity, often used in bathrooms, kitchens, and laundry rooms.

MR board Another term for moisture-resistant drywall.

Mud An informal term for joint compound.

Mudding An informal name for the job of taping and finishing drywall.

Mud tray A basin designed to hold joint compound during taping and finishing.

Nailer blocks Wooden framing members inserted vertically or horizontally within stud or joint bays to provide backing for drywall panels that do not break on studs, joists, or furring.

Nail plates See *Shields.*

Nail pop The phenomenon of nails or screws showing their heads after the drywall job has been taped, finished, and painted, usually caused by shrinkage in the framing.

NIOSH The National Institute for Occupational Safety and Health, a federal institute (part of the Centers for Disease Control and Prevention) that is responsible for conducting research and making recommendations for the prevention of work-related illness and injury.

Orange-peel finish A textured finish created by applying watered-down joint compound with an airless sprayer.

OSHA The Occupational Safety and Health Administration, a federal association (part of the Department of Labor) that is responsible for creating and enforcing workplace safety and health regulations.

Panel lifter A device that resembles a miniature seesaw, used to lift a drywall panel 1 or 2 inches off the floor and hold it in position for fastening.

Partition wall An interior wall that is not load-bearing.

Perforated paper tape Drywall tape with weep holes that allow joint compound to ooze through it.

Photographing When joint compound seams are visible through paint; curable by skim-coating.

Plasterboard A base material that provides a fire-resistant underlayment for trowel-applied plaster and has an absorbent face paper meant to draw water away from the freshly applied plaster to prevent slumping.

Plate See *Sole plate; Top plate.*

Plumb bob A pointed metal weight with a string used to determine vertical alignment.

Pole sander A 4-foot pole with a swiveling plate to which sandpaper is attached, used to sand high walls or ceilings.

Powder-actuated fasteners Masonry fasteners that are driven using an explosive charge.

Radius The measurement from the center of a circle to the circumference; half the diameter.

Rafter The sloping beams used to support the roof.

Ridge The highest point of a roof.

Ringed nail A nail that is threaded to resist withdrawal.

Sanding sponge Fine-grained (120-grit or finer) polyurethane block sponge used to sand drywall.

Scriber A V-shaped, caliper-like tool with a pencil on one arm, used to transfer the contour of an irregular or out-of-plumb wall to a drywall panel, which is then cut to fit.

Self-tapping screws Type S drywall screws that have flanged tips, which enable them to drill quickly through 20-gauge steel framing. Screws without these tips can drill out larger holes in the drywall, making them more difficult to finish.

Setting-type joint compound Available only in powdered form, this type hardens faster than drying-type compounds.

Sheetrock U.S. Gypsum Co.'s trade name for gypsum wallboard.

Shields Also called nail plates, these 1×2-inch metal plates are applied to stud edges to protect wires or pipe running within studs from drywall nails or screws.

Shoe stilts Typically 2 feet tall, these devices strap to the shoes and lower legs and allow you to work from the floor rather than a ladder.

Skim-coating The technique of rolling water-thinned joint compound onto a wall and then flattening it with a 20-inch knife to create a very thin, paint-like layer.

Soffit The underside of a wall bump-out or an overhang.

Sole plate Also called the sill plate or mudsill; the framing member that rests on the foundation and forms the base of the walls.

Sound-attenuating See *Sound-deadening*.

Sound-deadening Any process that has the intention of reducing sound transmission between rooms, such as two-layer applications of specialty drywall and acoustical sealant, metal channels, and sound-baffling stud configurations.

Spackle A trademarked name for a patching and repair compound.

Staggered studs A framing method whereby studs are installed 8 inches on center on a 2×6 bottom plate, with alternating studs flush with each side of the plate.

STC (Sound Transmission Class) A numerical rating that quantifies the ability of construction systems to deaden sound; the higher the number, the more effective the system.

Straight-handled knife A 10- or 12-inch-wide rigid knife backed with a wooden or plastic handle and used to feather out wide joint-compound seams.

Stud Vertical two-by lumber that extends from the bottom plate to the top plate of a wall.

Stud finder An electronic device used to determine stud locations behind a wall.

Subfloor Plywood or other board that is installed on joists to form the base of the finish flooring.

Substrate Any material that supports another material that is bonded over it, such as backer board for tile.

Surface-forming tool A hand-held rasp-like tool used to shave ⅛ inch or less from drywall edges.

Tape bender A tool designed to make a centered crease in drywall tape that is pulled through it.

Tape dispenser A drumlike tool clipped to the belt that dispenses drywall tape.

Tapered edge A slight, factory-milled bevel along both edges of a drywall panel's face side. When joined together, two such edges form a shallow V-shaped recess that allows tape and joint compound to be finished flush with the panel face.

Taping compound A drying-type joint compound used for the first coat or tape-embedding coat.

Taping knife A 5- or 6-inch scraper-like knife used to apply joint compound.

Textured roller A roller with a nap made from wire or plastic strands that leave a distinctive pattern in wet joint compound.

Toenailing Driving a nail at an angle into the face of a board so that it penetrates another board beneath or above it.

Tongue-and-groove panels Drywall panels with interlocking V-shaped edges.

Topping compound A drying-type joint compound used for the middle (filler) and/or finish coats.

Top plate The framing member(s) on top of a stud wall, upon which joists rest.

T-square A 4-foot aluminum square with a T-shaped fence. The fence has a lip on it that rests on the panel edge.

T-support See *Deadman*.

Type G screws Gypsum-type screws used to fasten drywall to drywall in a double-layer application.

Type S screws Steel-type screws used to fasten drywall to metal studs or furring.

Type W screws Wood-type screws used to fasten drywall to wood framing.

Type X gypsum board A drywall material that is fire resistant.

Utility knife A razor knife with a retractable, disposable blade used for cutting drywall.

Utility saw Also called a drywall or jab saw, it has a round handle and serrated knifelike blade and is used to cut holes for utility boxes, pipes, and ductwork. The pointed tip is thrust through the drywall to start the cut.

Vinyl-faced panel Predecorated drywall paneling that is attached using adhesive and special fasteners and that uses decorative plastic moldings for edge and joint treatments insead of joint compound and corner bead.

Wallboard Another generic term for drywall.

Water-resistant drywall See *Moisture-resistant drywall*.

Index

Index

Index

Photo Credits

Illustrations by Vincent Alessi, Clarke Barre (How-to and Tool Illustrations), Craig Franklin, Steve Karp (Line Art), James Randolph, Paul M. Schumm, Ray Skibinski.

All photography by David Baer of Smith-Baer Studios except where noted below.

pages 2–3: John Parsekian/CH **page 6:** *bottom* John Parsekian/CH **page 7:** *top* John Parsekian/CH; *bottom* courtesy of Georgia-Pacific **page 9:** *top* courtesy of U.S. Gypsum Corp.; *bottom* John Parsekian/CH **pages 11–12:** courtesy of National Gypsum Corp. **pages 13–15:** John Parsekian/CH **page 19:** courtesy of USG Drywall **page 24:** *top* courtesy of National Gypsum Corp.; *bottom* John Parsekian/CH **page 25:** courtesy of Stanley Tools **page 26:** *top* courtesy of USG Drywall; *bottom* courtesy of Sherwin Williams **page 27:** *both* courtesy of USG Drywall **page 28:** John Parsekian/CH **page 30:** *top left* courtesy of Celotex Corp.; *top right* & *bottom row* John Parsekian/CH **page 32:** John Parsekian/CH **page 34:** courtesy of Celotex Corp. **page 35:** *top* John Parsekian/CH **page 36:** *bottom* John Parsekian/CH **pages 37–38:** John Parsekian/CH **page 39:** courtesy of Alpha Tech, Inc. **page 40:** John Parsekian/CH **page 58:** *top* courtesy of U.S. Gypsum Corp. **page 61:** courtesy of U.S. Gypsum Corp. **page 64:** John Parsekian/CH **page 78:** John Parsekian/CH **page 80:** John Parsekian/CH **page 94:** John Parsekian/CH **page 104:** John Parsekian/CH **page 106:** John Parsekian/CH **pages 118–122:** courtesy of Bondex International, Inc. **page 124:** courtesy of U.S. Gypsum Corp. **pages 126–130:** John Parsekian/CH **pages 139–144:** John Parsekian/CH **page 145:** courtesy of Georgia-Pacific **page 146:** Richard Boun/Trim-Tex **page 147:** *both* courtesy of Armstrong **pages 148–151:** Neal Barrett/CH **pages 152–157:** Richard Boun/Trim-Tex **pages 158–159:** John Parsekian/CH **page 164:** John Parsekian/CH **pages 168–173:** John Parsekian/CH **page 174:** courtesy of National Gypsum Corp.

Metric Equivalents

Length

1 inch	25.4mm
1 foot	0.3048m
1 yard	0.9144m
1 mile	1.61km

Area

1 square inch	645mm²
1 square foot	0.0929m²
1 square yard	0.8361m²
1 acre	4046.86m²
1 square mile	2.59km²

Volume

1 cubic inch	16.3870cm³
1 cubic foot	0.03m³
1 cubic yard	0.77m³

Common Lumber Equivalents

Sizes: Metric cross sections are so close to their U.S. sizes, as noted below, that for most purposes they may be considered equivalents.

Dimensional lumber	1 x 2	19 x 38mm
	1 x 4	19 x 89mm
	2 x 2	38 x 38mm
	2 x 4	38 x 89mm
	2 x 6	38 x 140mm
	2 x 8	38 x 184mm
	2 x 10	38 x 235mm
	2 x 12	38 x 286mm
Sheet sizes	4 x 8 ft.	1200 x 2400mm
	4 x 10 ft.	1200 x 3000mm
Sheet thicknesses	¼ in.	6mm
	⅜ in.	9mm
	½ in.	12mm
	¾ in.	19mm
Stud/joist spacing	16 in. o.c.	400mm o.c.
	24 in. o.c.	600mm o.c.

Capacity

1 fluid ounce	29.57mL
1 pint	473.18mL
1 quart	0.95L
1 gallon	3.79L

Weight

1 ounce	28.35g
1 pound	0.45kg

Temperature

Fahrenheit = Celsius x 1.8 + 32
Celsius = Fahrenheit - 32 x 5⁄9

Nail Size and Length

Penny Size	Nail Length
2d	1"
3d	1¼"
4d	1½"
5d	1¾"
6d	2"
7d	2¼"
8d	2½"
9d	2¾"
10d	3"
12d	3¼"
16d	3½"

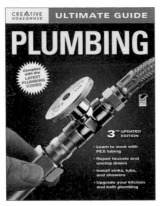

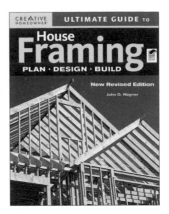

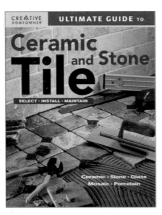

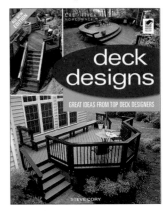
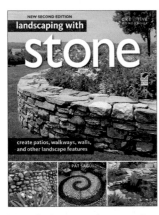

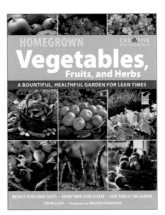